BEULAH HalleluYAH

MARCIA QUAINOO

ISBN 978-1-68570-563-3 (paperback)
ISBN 978-1-68570-564-0 (digital)

Christian Faith Publishing
832 Park Avenue
Meadville, PA 16335
www.christianfaithpublishing.com

Printed in the United States of America

THE NEXT CHAPTER

What better way to start this journey off by giving God Almighty thanks for how far He has brought me? To tell you the truth, I am so tired; however, there is absolutely no way I could've came home from work to rest without simply telling the Lord thank you. What better way to start off this new testament of my life by testifying about the miracle that I just witnessed today? Can you say miracle? A miracle, according to Google, is defined as "an effect or extraordinary event in the physical world that surpasses all known human or natural powers and is scribed to the supernatural cause."

I remember like it was yesterday. It was on August 22, 2019, one day before the first deadline given by US Citizenship and Immigration Services (USCIS) to me and my husband, but we had not received further instructions to the request for more evidence from USCIS that we had received via mail. There I was just getting off work and routinely going to check my mailbox in hopes of receiving the mail so we can obtain all that was being required of us to complete the first process in preparation for my husband to come home to me. Although USCIS has placed this claim to us, we were not really offended. Just weeks prior to the notice, we were told (by our lawyer) that our files were probably put on backlog. Now, what was only expected to take about six to nine months have been extended to eleven to fifteen months according to the report. So getting this notice on August 9, 2019, was such a blessing from God in our sight. However, when we had not received the request documents in the mail and knowing that we had a deadline of August 23, 2019, to meet, we were starting to get concerned. *Only one day left*, I was thinking. While on the phone with my daughter, hearing her calm and confident voice say, "Ma, it's going to be all right," soothed my spirit. As soon as I calmed down, there was the voice of the Holy Spirit. I could now hear Him speak clearly after I calmed down. I heard the Spirit say to me, "Look again one more time." I went on the USCIS site, and there it was, a message that read my case was approved—a complete miracle by God. Not "is," but "was approved"! Hallelujah! Our case was approved exactly ten days after receiving a request to submit more evidence. We were concerned about not getting the instructions for us to submit the requested evidence; however, the instructions never came. Look at God. It was already approved. Hallelujah! Glory to God! Only God can do it. The Lord had already gone before us. It was nothing short of a miracle. Glory to God.

"In everything give thanks for this is the will of God in Christ Jesus concerning you" (1 Thessalonians 5:18).

September 1, 2019

I am encouraged this morning by the Spirit of God to write. I am learning that God, my Father, is not and cannot be contained in a box. Putting God first in all things is the way! Jesus Christ, the Lord over my life, is the Rock of my salvation. Fear is no longer a factor in my life. I am redeemed by the blood of Jesus. I just finished reading Numbers 26 and Isaiah 4. The Word is my help. It is written also that the Word is a lamp to my feet and light to my path as recorded in the book of Psalm, not by power, nor by might, but by Your spirit, Lord. I am so thankful for the life that Jehovah has given me. I am so thankful for the teachings of the Holy Spirit. I surrendered my life unto the Lord. Years ago, the Lord Almighty told me, standing right in front of the mirror in my home, "No one will get the glory for what I have done in your life but me." Ever since the Lord had spoken those words to me, every time someone (no matter who they are) tried to take credit for God's anointing over my life, I shun away from them. The Lord is truly a miracle worker. Can He do it? Yes, He can do it. God is of the impossible. Can I do it? Yes, I can do all things through Christ who strengthens me as it is written.

Here I am, stepping out on faith with no electronic devices to keep up with the thoughts and ideas the Holy Spirit is giving me. No computer, no phone notes, and no recorder. Only a pen and a notepad. It feels so good to be able to just go back to the basics where it all started both physically and spiritually. All things work together for good of those who love the Lord as it is written. Amen.

September 3, 2019

Glory to God Almighty. Lord, You are good and Your mercy endures forever. I delight myself in You, Lord, as You give me the desire of my heart. There is none like You, Lord.

This day is so amazing. It is truly a blessing to be exploring the Lord and the beauty of His might. I am excited not only for my life or my family but also for the readers of my story. You get to live out my life experiences with me and my family through this new chapter of my life. I count it as a blessing. "Now faith" is my motto. I trust God with my whole life. No more fear will consume my life.

The Lord did not give us the spirit of fear. He has given us power, love, and a sound mind as it is written in the Word. I never knew love the way I am learning it now daily. All positive vibes. Here I am sitting on my bed smiling as I joyfully express myself through writing. Looking at one of my handbags across the room from me that reads, "Change your thoughts, change your life," this reminds me that I am walking in the right direction, walking by faith and not by sight. It is so amazing just how the Holy Spirit would bring the Word back to our memory if we would only allow Him to lead and guide us through the path of righteousness. Thank You, Lord. It is not enough to tell someone something that you heard. I no longer want to experience the minimum of the Lord's inheritance for my life. It is not the Lord's fault. All I ever had to do was just believe God's Word concerning my life. I will not fail this time. Say it with me, "I will not fail this time." Hallelujah!

Thank You, Lord. All the glory belongs to You. Yes, I am walking this path of righteousness by the grace of God. No longer am I just a hearer of God's Word, but a doer as well by the grace of God. Thank You, Holy Spirit, for Your guidance and comfort. It feels so good to be free. I am no longer bound. No more chains holding me down. Expressing myself through writing is a blessing. It feels so good. These are my thoughts and experiences, and I get to share them with you. Whether I am writing in first person or third person, who really cares when I feel freedom like the wind that blows. Thank You, Lord God, for Your Holy Spirit. What an experience to share. It is my prayer that you will be blessed by God as well.

I recall one Sunday, after church, one of the elders of the church came up to me and spoke some powerful words in my life. These words were, "Never do no more or no less than what God has given you to do." Yes, powerful. I have adopted this motto as well. What better motto to bring over to the new chapter of my life? I could have left this morning in my thoughts and actions because I found myself watching too much of YouTube concerning the immigration process in regard to the second process of National Visa Center (NVC) time frame. We have to watch our thoughts and focus on God's promises for our lives. I immediately got my mind together by thinking positive and rejecting those negative thoughts. No more what-ifs for me. It's what the Word says concerning my desires of my heart and God's will for my life. Amen.

Oh give thanks unto the Lord: For he is good: for his mercy endureth for ever. (Psalm 136:1)

Again I say to you that if two of you agree on earth concerning anything that they ask, it will be done for them by my Father in Heaven. (Matthew 18:19)

And whatever things you ask in prayer,
believing, you will receive. (Matthew 21:22)

Yes, God has done it before, and yes, God will do it again and again. There is no failing in God. There are So many testimonies, yet I am only going to share a couple today. "God's timing is the best timing," as my husband often says. I am continuously hearing my beloved husband speak those words to me even though he is not physically here with me right now. I am so sure that those words are in the Word somewhere in some form or another because they have brought such life to my life when I needed it the most. As a matter of fact, I thank You, Holy Spirit, for reminding me of the fruit of the Spirit, patience. Exercising those words helps me to have patience to wait on the manifestation of God's promises in my life. I pray that you are blessed also as you journey with me to see what that Lord has done.

Over the last three weeks, we lost our eldest brother, and my daughter was in two car accidents during the same time. It was trying but not devastated because of our stance in our Lord. Our brother's homegoing was a celebration because the Lord had prepared the family through his testimony before the Lord transitioned him home to be with Him. Also, for our daughter, she sustained no broken bones. She was a bit shaken emotionally but no major injuries, and she just needed some reassurance and loving support. Hallelujah! We give God the glory.

September 5, 2019

Thank You, Lord, King of kings, Lord of lords, and Alpha and Omega, the beginning and the end, the only one and living God that supplies all my needs. Amen. Glory glory glory! The Lord God is good. I am confident in the Word of God. It feel so good to meditate and explore the Word of God. Who would have ever known that the Word is this good lest they have tasted it themselves? Oh, taste and see that the Lord is good as it is written.

I am elated for this new chapter of my life. It feels so good to experience it with you. My only hope is that your lives will be changed as you accept Jesus Christ as your Lord and Savior. Allowing Jesus to be Lord over our lives is the best gift that we can give to ourselves. Thank you, Lord. I am a believer. Ask me who am I and I will say boldly, "I am a believer in Christ Jesus as Lord of my life." Hallelujah! There has truly been a changing of guards. The Holy Spirit is bountifully working through my life. The holy angels of the living God have gone on before me. I am confident in God's Word. Thank You, Lord. The joy of the Lord is my strength as it is written. It feels so good to love on my Father in heaven.

One might ask, "How can she be that happy?" I would tell you, "You just have to know my story." However, that's my past. That is another story and is not included in this new chapter. Glory to God! Old things have passed away; behold, all things are made new through Christ Jesus as it is written.

September 10, 2019

Thank You, Lord. Glory to God. It's another day that You have kept me, Lord. The last few days have definitely been some trying days, but I am committed to keeping my vow to keep our conversation positive and keep it moving toward my dream. Lord, You are good and Your mercy endureth forever. Sitting on side of my bed this morning, looking at my handbag that reads, "Change your thoughts, change your life." It's all about building, sowing, and applying God's principles to the new chapter in my life. It's about being a hearer and doer of God's Word. It's about building my faith in the Word of God by staying committed to reading and communing with the Lord Almighty. I am determined to keeping my relationship with my Father in heaven fresh. He said in His Word that He is my Friend. When it comes down to natural friends, one always has to contend with not being good enough. With the Lord, the Word says that His grace is sufficient. Isn't that awesome? When we are in Christ, He loves us through it all. In Christ, we are enough because His grace is sufficient in our lives. Who wouldn't love a God like my God? Say it, "I am more than enough because God's grace is sufficient in my life." Hallelujah! Glory to God. So the Word today is "Keep it moving, stay committed, and trust God for His promise for our lives and desires." Amen.

As it is written, if we delight ourselves in him, he will give us our heart desires. Yes, some days are trying days but know that we are victorious through Christ Jesus. No time for doubting. I know too much about God. There is no time or blessing in looking back. March forward saints of God. We can do this together.

September 15, 2019

Thank You. Thank You. Thank You, Lord. Lord God, You are so Faithful. All we have to do is trust You, God Almighty; such an awesome Father You are. Thank You for bringing Your Word back to my memory. Yes, Lord, I hear You clearly this morning. "Seek the Lord while He can be found," is what I am hearing. Yes, Lord. Yes yes yes! This word is for the masses, including myself. Hallelujah!

As I recall earlier this morning, when You first gave me this word, I became distracted by social media when I started to Google what You had just given me. This was my firsthand experience on just how quickly it is to be distracted by the cares of this world. I was reminded, "Marcia, stay focused on what the Lord has given you." God's Word is absolutely precious and is meant to be shared because the Lord is soon to return.

Oh, how I love the Lord. Although I was distracted, You, Father, had mercy on me and allowed me to hear Your voice again by Your grace. Thank You, Lord, for bringing Your Word back to my memory. Lord, You keep doing great things for me. I will tell it wherever I go. So today and every day for the rest of my life, I will be committed to staying focused and seeking You, Father, while You can be found. I am so happy. I will remember this private, intimate moment with You even if it was in the bathroom on the commode while praying and singing to You, Lord Almighty. "Seek ye the Lord while he may be found, call ye upon him while he is near" (Isaiah 55:6).

Amen. Hallelujah!

September 19, 2019

Thank You, Lord. All the glory belongs to You, Lord. Wow! You are so amazing. My soul rejoices in You, Lord. I'm dreaming big. I am dreaming big-time. I hear You, Lord. "It is already taken care of," was the word of the Lord to me in my dream.

I remember living in a rental property, just as I am now, in my dream. It was me and my husband's home. Yes, my husband had come home. Thank You, Lord. In this dream, the Lord was revealing to me different situations that I had been dealing with such as people that had been secretly offended by me. The Lord showed me their hearts toward me and why they had taken offense, but I knew, by the spirit of the Lord, they were just blinded by their fears. One once called me friend but now was blinded by their fear of who I was becoming in Christ. They were also blinded by their insecurities that had been tormenting them secretly. Who would have ever known? Only by the Spirit of God, the true intent of man's heart is revealed. The Lord Almighty knows our hearts. Fear is a spirit. The Lord has not given us a spirit of fear; but, power, love, and a sound mind as it is written. So if the Lord did not give us the spirit of fear, whose spirit are we carrying? I thank God that the story did not end there. My soul rejoices. For every problem that a true worshiper experiences, there is a solution in the Word of God. Hallelujah!

In this dream, the same people that had seen me through the eyes of flesh now had come to my home to experience the power of God. Although the initial intent wasn't good, the power of God was at work. Thank You, Lord. Although the initial intent was not good, *love* was in the air. Although the initial intent was not good, my mind is sound. The spirit of fear might have been the driving force; however, when fear encountered power, love, and a sound mind, fear could no longer survive in that kind of atmosphere. The Lord had already taken care of it by the promises of His Word. Hallelujah! What the devil meant for bad, God had already turned it around. All for the glory of God. The Lord will cause our enemies to be at peace with us. Thank you, Lord!

Also, in this dream, our home had started flooding with water. A water pipe had burst, and water had started to appear and fill the hallway. The water was in its beginning stages of spreading into our home. I saw this man that was walking with the presence of God upon him. He was walking in the office of a priest. He was walking throughout our home. I had no idea where he came from, but I walked over to him to tell him about our situation because I recognized him as a landlord. We were living in his home. When I approached him to tell him of our problem, he immediately and firmly looked over at me and said, "It has already been taken care of." I looked around, and there were no busted water pipes. Amazingly enough, there was PEACE in our home. Hallelujah!

When the spirit of fear encounters the true love of God, it produces PEACE. Thank You, Lord. The Lord will even make our enemies be at peace with us. We fight not against flesh and blood as it is written. No weapon formed against us shall prosper as it is written. The battle belongs to the Lord as it is written. God is LOVE. Thank You, Lord, for victorious dreams.

The Lord's words to me in the dream were, "It has already been taken care of." Such powerful words. Such powerful message. It reminds me of a passage in the book of Isaiah 65:24: "Before we even call upon the Lord, He has already answered us." For every problem for those that worship the Lord in spirit and truth, there is an answer that already has been decided by God that works in our favor. Hallelujah! If it is our enemies, God has already taken care of it. If it is our heart's desire, God has already taken care of it. If it is our home, God has already taken care of it. Whatever concerns us, both hidden and seen, God has already taken care of it. Hallelujah! Even these earthly borrowed vessels that we now live in, God is concerned, and He has already taken care of it. Glory to God for dreaming big this morning. Increase, Lord! Hallelujah!

September 21, 2019

Good morning, Holy Spirit. Hallelujah! Thank You, Lord. I praise Your, holy name. You know my name, Lord. I am more than a conqueror through Christ Jesus as it is written. Jesus Christ is the Way, Truth, and Life as it is written. This is my story. This is my song. Hallelujah!

I woke up this morning with anticipation and believing God for a great day. Here I am sitting on side of my bed, meditating on the song "Grace and Mercy." Lord knows we all need His grace and mercy. Lord, thank You for reminding me that it is Your grace and mercy that have brought us this far and will lead us through. This is my story, and this is my song, praising my Savior all day long. All I can hear this morning are songs. Thank you, Holy Spirit, for ministering to me in song this morning. Lord, you are so awesome.

One song that I woke up singing this morning, "Grace and Mercy," is exactly what I needed. I absolutely have no time to look back on yesterday, for this is the day that the Lord has made; and I will rejoice and be glad in it as it is written, binding every negative thought, concern, or fear in the name of Jesus. I remember how You brought me over, Lord. Never will I forget January 2017. That day, I was hopeless, helpless, and broken. I had disappointed You, Father in heaven, once again; but it was You, Lord, who brought me through. I give You the praise, Lord. My new chapter in life is about giving You the praise, Father in heaven. Thank You, Lord, again for Your grace and mercy. Thank You for all You have done for me, Lord. Hallelujah!

September 22, 2019

Yes, I got this with the help of the Lord. I must admit every day has not been the best day, but every day has been a blessed day. Yes, I want to keep it real to my readers. At the same time, I am determined to live out my best life for the rest of my life. You, the readers, get the opportunity to walk with me through this path. By the Spirit of God, we all can do this. I am aware that my thoughts can be very random at times. It can sometimes seem like I am all over the place. Well, you know what? You are exactly right about it. I definitely want to live my truth. You get the opportunity to experience the growth and determination that I am experiencing as well. Can we all do it? Yes, we can. We can actually grow together.

I have given God the praise early this morning. I am focused on praising Him throughout this day. I will not apologize for thanking God all throughout my writings. If it had not been for the Lord, where would I be? I know that I would not be getting the opportunity to experience such joy in my life nor share it with you all. Yes, I am so hopeful for my future as well as yours. It is my prayer that the Lord get the glory out of these writings, and you all testify that God is good and His mercy endureth forever. So let us kick the devil in his neck. Yes, in his neck. LOL. Say it with me. You know the words, "I can do all things through Christ who strengthens me," as it is written. Hallelujah!

HERE WE GO! READY, SET, GO!

THREE THINGS I WANT US TO REMEMBER:

1. TRUST GOD.
2. KNOW THAT WE ARE A TEAM, ONE IN CHRIST.
3. IMAGINE, BELIEVE, AND RECEIVE.

TRUST GOD

Trust in the Lord with all thine heart; and lean not unto thine own understanding. In all thy ways acknowledge him, and he shall direct thy paths. (Proverbs 3:5–6)

Create in me a clean heart, O God; and renew a right spirit within me. Cast me not away from thy presence; and take not thy Holy Spirit from me. Restore unto me the Joy of thy salvation; and uphold me with thy free Spirit. Then will I teach transgressors thy ways; and sinners shall be converted unto thee. (Proverbs 51:10–13)

These writings are about living out our best life through Christ who strengthens us. How can we do that if we have not received Him as our Lord and Savior? How is it possible to trust God when he is not Lord over our lives? How? How can we teach transgressors if we are still bound by our transgressions and sins? How?

> The heart is deceitful above all things, and desperately wicked: who can know it. I the Lord search the heart, I try the reins, even to give every man according to his ways, and according to the fruit of his doings. (Jeremiah 17:9–10)

> In the beginning was the Word, and the Word was with God, and the Word was God. The same was in the beginning with God. All things were made by him; and without him was not anything made that was made. In him was life; and the life was the light of men. And the light shineth in darkness, and the darkness comprehended it not. (John 1:1–5)

> And if Christ be in you, the body is dead because of sin; but the Spirit is Life because of righteousness. But if the Spirit of him that raised up Jesus from the dead dwell in you, he that raised up Christ from the dead shall also quicken your mortal bodies by his spirit that dwelleth in you. Therefore, brethren, we are debtors, not to the flesh, to live after the flesh. For if ye live after the flesh, ye shall die: but if ye through the spirit do mortify the deeds of the body, ye shall live. For as many as are led by the Spirit of God, they are the sons of God. For ye have not received the Spirit on Bondage again to fear; but ye have received the Spirit of adoption, whereby we cry, Abba, Father. The Spirit itself beareth witness with our

spirit, that we are the children of God. And if children, then heirs; heirs of God, and joint heirs with Christ; if so be that we suffer with him, that we may be also glorified together. For I reckon that the sufferings of the present time not worthy to be compared with the glory which shall be revealed in us. (Romans 8:10–18)

But what saith it? The Word is nigh thee, even in thy mouth, and in thy heart: that is, the word of faith, which we preach: That if thou shalt confess with thy mouth the Lord Jesus, and shalt believe in thine heart that God hath raised him from the dead thou shalt be saved. For with the heart man believeth unto righteousness; and with the mouth confession is made unto salvation. For the scripture saith, whosoever believeth on him shall not be ashamed. (Romans 10:9–11)

September 25, 2019

Thank You, God Almighty. Father, You are such an awesome God. Thank You, Jesus. Holy Spirit, I acknowledge Your presence this morning. Father, I hear You. I thank God, my Father in heaven, for the foundation of His Word. I feel liberated, and it feels so good to trust God. I know who I am now in Christ. It was necessary. Every trial, every disappointment, every rejection, every persecution, every fall was all necessary. I can see clearly now. Thank You, Lord. I feel like Joshua and Caleb when they returned, along with the other leaders, to report what they had seen in the promised land. Although they were the minority, among the other leaders, they knew who they were. They knew the power of God and what God can do. Most of all, they trusted God's Word for their lives in spite of their weakness. We serve the same God that Joshua and Caleb served. The Lord God is the same yesterday, today, and forevermore as it is written. I am excited to be able to experience God's promise for my life with you, the reader.

It is my prayer that, by now, you have experienced the presence of God and have accepted Him as your personal Lord and Savior just as I have. I pray that you have put all of your trust in God our Father in heaven. I pray that you are reading and studying God's Word daily so that the proper foundation of God's Word will be settled in your lives. I feel the Lord walking with us through this journey. It is truly an honor to walk with Him. He is my Friend. Let us get to know Him better through the Word of God. The Lord never expected the Israelites to possess their inheritance of the promised land of Canaan without Him. He never expected them to forget who He was. Just as today, the Lord Almighty has promised us our rightful inheritance, eternal life, through Christ Jesus. We can do nothing without the Lord on our side. He does not intend for us to cross over alone. He is right here all the way. Are you excited? I am so excited because I can feel Him moving inside of me. Thank You, Lord. Thank You for Your Holy Spirit. Thank You, Lord, for knowing my weakness and for empowering me with Your spirit to overcome all obstacles set before me. I trust You, Father in heaven. Hallelujah!

And lest I should be exalted above measure through the abundance of the revelations, there was given to me a thorn in the flesh, the messenger of Satan to buffet me, lest I should be exalted above measure. For this thing I besought the Lord thrice, that it might depart from me. And he said unto me, my grace is sufficient for thee: for my strength is made perfect in weakness. Most gladly therefore will I rather glory in my infirmities, that the power of Christ may rest upon me. Therefore, I take pleasure in infirmities, in reproaches, in necessities, in persecutions, in distresses for Christ's sake: for when I am weak, then am I strong. (2 Corinthians 12:7–10)

Trust in the Lord with all thine heart, and lean not unto thine own understanding. In all thy ways acknowledge him, and he shall direct thy path. (Proverbs 3:5–6)

Wow wow wow! These scriptures have blessed me this morning. As I told you before, you are getting the opportunity to experience my walk with the Lord. I believe God's Word for my life. What do you believe God for in your lives? What has our Lord promised you? Do you trust Him? We are more than conquerors through Christ Jesus as it is written. We are the head and not the tail, the lenders and not the borrowers. Do we really know who we are? We can inherit God's promises for our lives. My husband always tells me, "Do not mind the naysayers." My husband encourages me when adversities try to distract me from God's promises. He always reminds me of the Word of God spoken in my life. So let me encourage you as well. Again, let us trust God because our strength is mad perfect in weakness as it is written. Hallelujah!

WE ARE A TEAM

WHOLLY FOLLOW CHRIST

> Save Caleb the son of Jephunneh; he shall see it, and to him will I give the land that he hath trodden upon, and to his children, because he hath wholly followed the Lord. (Deuteronomy 1:36)

> But Joshua the son of Nun, which standeth before thee, he shall go in thither: encourage him: for he shall cause Israel to inherit it. (Deuteronomy 1:38)

Are we leaders that follow Christ? Ooch! By example, Moses led the people of God who were complaining and murmuring, and this caused a certain kind of response that resulted in him and those children of God designated by God not to enter into the land promised by God. Only God will get the glory for what He has done. A life of doubt, disobedience, murmuring, or complaining will keep us from the blessings and promises that God has for us.

There is so much to learn from the scriptures of God. Faith comes by hearing, hearing by the Word of God as it is written. The opposite of faith is fear and doubt. This is not my portion. Please, join me on this road to our promised land. There will be some, even today, that will hear the Word of God and the testimonies and still not reap a harvest, even leaders, not because they do not have the ability to lead, but because of the rumblings of murmuring and complaining will distract them from their inheritance. I declare this will not be our portion nor testimony. Hallelujah!

"Thy Word is a lamp unto my feet, and a light unto my path" (Psalm 119:105).

I love the writings of Moses in the Word of God. They are examples for us to live by today. No one could do what Moses was called to do but Moses. Even in his weakness, the Lord God Almighty held him accountable to speak His Word to the pharaoh and lead the people of God to the promised land. God Almighty didn't initially call for Aaron and Joshua; however, because of his mercy and will for His people, the Word had already gone before them and will not return to the Lord Thy God void. Hallelujah!

Again, the writings of Moses tell us that he was some kind of great leader appointed by God. When talking about teamwork, there must be a great team leader. When you have a great team leader, even in those days in the wilderness, there will be increase and growth. It was evident that God's hand was on Moses and the people of God. Glory to God. The Lord had brought them through both night and day. In the book of Deuteronomy, mainly in chapter 2, God reminded the people of God just how He had been there all the time. Glory to God!

> For the Lord thy God hath blessed thee in all the works of thy hand. He knoweth thy walking through this great wilderness: these forty years the Lord thy God hath been with thee; thou hast lacked nothing. (Deuteronomy 2:7)

> Ye have compassed this mountain long enough: turn you northward. (Deuteronomy 2:3)

PAUSE! MOMENT OF SILENCE.

As I sit here in my bed reading, studying, and meditating on God's Word, I am literally at awe at just how great God is. Our Father makes no mistakes. I was just reading in the Word of God a couple of days ago on God's sufficient grace and how our strength is made perfect in weakness as it is written. All is not lost. Moses was and is still a part of God's plan. Though he didn't get the chance to lead the people of God into the promise land, he was chosen by God and followed the Lord and led the children of Israel through the wilderness, and the promise land was in his view. Hallelujah!

For a moment there, I started to get sad by the notion that Moses couldn't enter the promised land. God! Hallelujah! Moses was a powerful man, but in all, he was still just a man used by God. Moses was and still is God's man, and no one will get the glory but God Almighty for what God had already done through Christ. Even though Moses was a team leader in the sight of God's people, Moses was impulsive. All is not lost. Thank God for the writings of Moses. Such great example to follow, but Jesus Christ is the perfect example to follow. Through Christ we are all becoming leaders. In that saying, we all have to know how to lead and follow. A great leader is also a great follower of Christ. Christ Jesus is the way to our Father in heaven as it is written. There is no other way except the way to destruction. Your choice. Choose wisely as I have. Hallelujah!

> For what the law could not do, in that it was weak through the flesh, God sending His own Son in the likeness of sinful flesh, and for sin, condemned sin in the flesh: that the righteousness of the law might be fulfilled in us, who walk not after the flesh, but after the spirit. (Romans 8:3–4)

> For as many as are led by the Spirit of God, they are the sons of God. For ye have not received the spirit of bondage again to fear, but ye have received the spirit of adoption whereby we cry, "Abba Father. The Spirit itself beareth witness

with our spirit, that we are the children of God.
And if children, then heirs; heirs of God, and
joint-heirs with Christ; if so be that we suffer
with him, that we may be also glorified together.
(Romans 8:14–17)

Therefore if any man be in Christ, he is a
new creature: old things are passed away; behold
all things are become new. And all things are of
God, who hath reconciled us to himself by Jesus
Christ, and hath given to us the ministry of reconciliation. To wit, that God was in Christ, rec-
onciling the world unto himself, not imputing
their trespasses unto them; and hath committed
unto us the word of reconciliation. Now then we
are ambassadors for Christ, as though God did
beseech you by us; we pray you in Christ's stead,
be ye reconciled to God. For he hath made him
to be sin for us, who knew no sin; that we might
be made the righteousness of God in Him. (2
Corinthians 5:17–21)

THANKSGIVING

Thank You, thank You, thank You, Lord God! You are so awesome. Yet again, You have shown up in a powerful way. You are a rewarder of those who seek You, my Lord. This is Your day, Lord, and I celebrate life on today. My soul is rejoicing this morning. It is truly a blessing to be a part of Your team, Father in heaven. It is truly a blessing to be able to share Your good news, that "Jesus is Lord" over my life. Knowing that I am not alone on the journey is so gratifying. It gives me hope. Thank You, Holy Spirit, for comforting me.

Father, Your Word says, "Let us hold fast the profession of our faith without wavering (for he is faithful that promised)" (Hebrews 10:23).

> Cast not away therefore your confidence, which has great recompence of reward. For ye have need of patience, that, after ye have done the will of God, ye might receive the promise. For yet a little while, and he that shall come will come, and will not tarry. (Hebrews 10:35–37)

> But without faith it is impossible to please him: for he that cometh to God must believe that he is, and that he is a rewarder of them that diligently seek him. (Hebrews 11:6)

I hear You today, Lord, loud and clear. I praise You, Lord. All the glory belongs to You, Lord. Thank You, Father in heaven. "Hallowed be Thy Name. Thy kingdom come on earth as it is in heaven." I thank You for Your daily bread. There is none like You, Father. You reign in my life. You are unpredictable. Father, You are untraceable like the wind. You are omnipresence, everywhere at the same time. There is liberty in Your Word. Your Word became flesh and dwelt among us as it is written. Lord Jesus, You know all about our pain and struggles. For You alone, Lord, have paid the price that we might receive You as Lord and Savior over our lives. This life that I now live, I live through Jesus Christ, my Lord and Savior. Hallelujah!

Father God in heaven, there is no failing in You. I hope in You. I trust You. I follow You wholly. I shall reap the harvest that You have for me. My family is blessed. My body is blessed. My finances are blessed. I thank You, Lord God. Hallelujah! There is none like You. Here I am, Lord. Use me to for Your service. I just wanted to take this moment this morning to thank You, Father God, in heaven for changing my life. I will continue to seek Ye first the kingdom of heaven. I will diligently seek You, Lord. I am a recipient of Your promise. With You leading me, Holy Spirit, I will not fail. I shall arrive at my destination on time. Thank You, Lord!

I will praise thee, O Lord, with my whole heart, I will shew forth all they marvellous works. I will be glad and rejoice in thee: I will sing praise to thy name, O thou most High. When mine enemies are turned back, they shall fall and perish at thy presence. For thou has maintained my right and my cause thou satest in the throne judging right. Thou hast rebuked the heathen, thou has destroyed the wicked, thou hast put out their name for ever and ever. O thou enemy, destructions are come to a perpetual end: and thou hast destroyed cities; their memorial is perished with them. But the Lord shall endure forever: he hath prepared his throne for judgement. And he shall

judge the world in righteousness, he shall minister judgement to the people in uprightness. The
Lord also will be a refuge for the oppressed, a refuge in times of trouble. And they that know thy
name will put their trust in thee: for thou, Lord,
hast not forsaken them that seek thee. Sing praise
to the Lord, which dwelleth in Zion: declare
among the people his doings. (Psalm 9:1–11)

For thou, Lord has not forsaken them that
seek thee. (Psalm 9:10b)

But if from thence thou shalt seek the Lord
thy God, thou shalt find him, if thou seek him
with all thy heart and with all thy soul. When
thou art in tribulation, and all these things are
come upon thee, even in the latter days, if thou
turn to the Lord thy God, and shalt be obedient
unto his voice (For the Lord thy God is a merciful God); he will not forsake thee, neither destroy
thee, nor forget the covenant of thy fathers which
he sware unto them. (Deuteronomy 4:29–31)

Wow! What a powerful word today that the Holy Spirit is ministering to me. I hear You, Lord. "Seek me," saith the Spirit of God. I
confess that my latter days are greater. If I had ten thousand tongues,
I still would not be able to thank God for all that He is doing right
now. My hope is in You, Lord. It is such a blessing to be experiencing
the joy of the Lord with You, the readers. We are a team that Christ
has established in these latter days. Jesus is soon to come. I am convinced and glad about it. I seek and desire to fulfill the will of God
by the Spirit of God. It is not God's Will that one soul be lost. Do it,
Lord. Change our testimonies to line up with Your will for our lives
through Christ Jesus. I believe God. No turning back, no matter the
cost. Jesus paid the price. Hallelujah!

Thank You, Lord! Hallelujah! There is none like You, Father. You know my name. I belong to You, Lord. I am Your own. Thank You for my family. Thank You for fighting our battles. We believe You. We trust You, Lord. Thank You for the turnaround. Bless Your name, Father. Glory belongs to You, Lord. As I lay here in my bed, I am reflecting how good God is. The power of God is real. Lord, I praise You, Father. No one can do the things that You have already done. Just on yesterday, You, Lord, have turned the story of my family. Thank You for renewing relationships. Thank You for traveling grace. Thank You for the financial increase. Thank You, Lord, for Your grace on our jobs. Thank You, Lord, for grace in our marriage. I'm singing, "I am determined to follow Jesus, no turning back, no turning back."

IMAGINE/BELIEVE/RECEIVE

The best thing about writing my journey is the fact that I do not have to worry about feeling condemned or not being good enough in man's view. Whether first, second, or third person, it doesn't matter. At this point, I am not worrying about my grammar. Those that my journey is meant to bless will be blessed. Hallelujah! God is so awesome. He is amazing. Our Father is faithful to His Word. Thank You, Lord, for Your power. Holy Spirit, continue to lead the way, and I will follow for Your glory, Lord.

"Delight thyself also in the Lord, and he shall give thee the desires of thine heart. Commit thy way unto the Lord, trust also in him; and he shall bring it to pass" (Psalm 37:4–5).

I am totally at awe this morning. I have quoted this verse several times, but this morning, there is a new meaning in this scripture. Thank You, Holy Spirit! The word "also" in this particular passage stands out to me. The word also tells me that the writer is also wanting me to pay close attention to preceding words that were spoken before this word. In other words, "And we know that all things work together for good to them that love God, to them who are the called according to his purpose" (Romans 8:28).

Let's go back to the passage in Psalm 37:4 and the word "also." The beginning of this scripture is "delight thyself also" and the keyword again is "also." So I have to ask myself what the words that precede "delight thyself also" are. It is written, "Trust in the Lord, and do good, so shalt thou dwell in the land and verily thou shalt be fed" (Psalm 37:3).

Let's talk about the desires of our heart. We have to ask ourselves what we desire. How can we obtain them? By definition, a desire is "a strong feeling of wanting to have something or wishing for something to happen." By definition, imagine is "to form a mental image or concept of." Other words to imagine is to visualize or envisage.

Right at this moment, my desire is that you understand what I really want to say and find the right words to say by expressing it in writing with hope that you and I both will be blessed by it for years to come. So, with less words, what is my desire? My desire is for you and me to be blessed. You, the reader, may have to grasp the whole concept of what I am saying.

The blessings of God are not always linked to our understanding. Some things, we will not be able to grasp or comprehend initially, but by the power of God, we can trust God and know that it's all working for our good.

The Bible is probably known to be the most complex and controversial book on this land. I remember years ago, when I first started desiring to be close to God, I couldn't understand or my face stayed with a perplexed look. I could feel the lines in the middle of my forehead growing bigger every time I open the Bible to read. No one told me to expect that reaction. No one told me to pray first and then invite the Holy Spirit to guide me.

I can remember just like it was yesterday. It was the year 2000. There I was driving down Cherry Street on my way home, repeating, "Thank you, Jesus," over and over again. Suddenly, there was a burning sensation that come over me, and I felt the unction to just let go and speak in unknown tongues. It was the very moment that I had been desiring for—intimacy with my Lord, my Father in heaven, through the Spirit of God. There He was "the evidence of" what I had been hoping for, or shall I say desiring. Hallelujah! Glory to God Almighty! None like You, Lord! Thank You, Jesus! Even today, at this moment, I feel the power of God in me rumbling and ready!

> Now faith is the substance of things hope for, the evidence of things not seen. (Hebrews 11:1)

> Through faith we understand that the
> worlds was framed by the word of God so that
> things which are seen were not made of things
> which do appear. (Hebrews 11:2)
>
> Cast not away therefore your confidence,
> which that great recompense of reward. For ye
> have need for patience, that, after ye have done
> the will of God, ye might receive the promise.
> For yet a little while, and he that shall come will
> come, and will not tarry. Now the just shall live
> by Faith, but if any man draw back, my soul
> shall have no pleasure in him, But we are not of
> them who draw back unto perdition, but of them
> that believe to the savings of the soul. (Hebrews
> 10:35–39)

> So then faith cometh by hearing, and hear-
> ing by the Word of God. (Romans 10:17)

October 5, 2019

Good morning, Holy Spirit. Lord, You are amazing. I just finished reading the last passage from yesterday, and it just blessed me
again. I thought to myself, *So amazing You are, Lord!* If I were an
English teacher, I wouldn't change a thing at this point. What matters most, our grammar or our soul? Bread of heaven, feed us Your
Word and fill us with Your Power, Lord Almighty.

> But when the Comforter is come, whom
> I will send unto you from the Father, even the
> Spirit of truth, which proceedeth from the
> Father, he shall testify of me: And ye also shall
> bear witness, because ye have been with me from
> the beginning. (John 15:26–27)

> Nevertheless I tell you the truth, It is expedient for you that I go away; for if I go not away, the Comforter will not come unto you; But, if I depart, I will send him unto you. And when he is come, he will reprove the world of sin, and of righteousness, and of judgement. (John 16:7–8)

I know now that the Lord has been with me all the time. Looking back over my life as I journeyed through this weary land, God has truly been faithful to me. I know and believe that for you as well. It is evident to me. You are still reading my story, and that lets me know that the Holy Spirit is moving here. Remember, my desire is that we are all blessed even more by this journey. Let's keep believing God for increase. Let's keep believing God for His promise. It is my desire that you too can see God's promise over your life. What has God promised you? Can you imagine? Is it in view?

We know God's promise when it is to bring Him and Him alone glory. Hallelujah! I am not talking about our selfish desires. I am talking about the promises of God that will bring glory to Him alone. In other words, our desires should line up with God's will for our lives whether that be marriage, children, prosperity, relationships, physical appearance, or land. Remember, as believers of Christ Jesus and witnesses, all that we desire and do is for the glory of God.

As believers, our lives did not start when our mothers conceived us. Our lives started with Christ before conception. According to the Word of God, "And ye also shall bear witness, because ye have been with me from the beginning" (John 16:27). Yes! Jesus was there and still is here for us. He was there all the time. There is a famous song titled "He Was There All the Time." Hallelujah! I feel the Spirit of God. We have a reason to celebrate God! We must trust His Word. We must keep the Faith. He is Lord of lords, King of kings, and Lord of hosts.

October 6, 2019

Thank You, holy Father, Abba Father, Miracle Worker, and Promise Keeper, for all You have done for me. There is none like You. Hallelujah! Glory to You, Father in heaven. Thank You for eyes to see. My promise is within my view. Thank You, Jesus! Lord, You lead, and I will follow. Amen.

Looking back over my life, I realized that the Lord has never forsaken me. He has been with me all the time. I tell people often that I have been in church all my life, but church has not always been in me. That's another story for another time. This journey here is all about the glory of God revealed through the Holy Spirit. It's all about lifting up the mighty name of Jesus. Oh, how precious is the blood of Jesus. When no one else was there, my Lord was there. No matter what the trials were, I was determined not to give up. It was all necessary. I do regret some of my choices, but I thank God for His grace and mercy. I couldn't see then, but now, I can see much clearer.

In 2000, there was a turning point in my life, but not the turning point of my life. "What are you saying, Marcia?" I am saying that 2000 was the year that I received the gift of the Holy Spirit as evidenced by speaking in tongues as spoken of as I had learned, but I was still denying the power. I wanted the intimacy with the Lord so bad. I had imagined what it would feel like for so long to speak in unknown tongues to the Lord, but I was unaware that I wasn't totally submitted to the will of God.

The Bible says, "Having a form of godliness, but denying the power thereof: from such turn away" (2 Timothy 3:5).

There I was, in 2000, high off the experience but still lacked intimacy with the Lord. By this time, I had been trying to study the Word without the power of God and didn't even know it. I had imagined and desired the gift of speaking in tongues, but when what I had hoped for came to pass, it really didn't dawn on me that the Holy Spirit was a person whom I had to submit to, and the gift of speaking in tongues was a gift of the Holy Spirit given to intercede on my behalf to help me commune with the Father. In my eyes, I thought I had submitted to the Father, but it was in my own power and not by the Spirit. I didn't realize I was so focused on the experience rather than the change as a result of exercising the gift that I had finally received from the Lord. The gift was there all the time. I just had to open my heart up, have faith, ask, receive, and SUBMIT for the glory of God to be revealed. Amen. Like some believers today, I had become religious rather that spiritual. We have to be full of the Spirit of God so that we do not fulfill the lust of our flesh as it is written. Amen.

> What doth it profit my brethren, though a man say he hath faith and have not works can faith save him? If a brother or sister be naked, and destitute of daily food, and one of you say unto them, depart in peace be ye warmed and filled; notwithstanding ye give them not those things which are needful to the body; what doth it profit? Even so faith, if it hath not works, is dead, being alone. Yea, a man may say, thou hast faith, and I have works: shew me thy faith without thy work, and I will shew thee my faith by my works thou believest that there is one God; thou doest will: the devils also believe, and tremble. But wilt thou know, O vain man, that faith without works is dead? (James 2:14–20)

What now? I had hope for God's gift of speaking in tongues. It manifested as I had hoped. Now what? What happens when we hope for something so long and when it comes what now? I didn't know to ask God to prepare me for what I desired. It's not enough to have a gift from God and not know how to exercise that gift for the glory of God.

> Was not Abraham our father justified by works, when he had offered Isaac his son upon the Alter? Seest thou how faith wrought with his works, and by works was faith made perfect? And

the scripture was fulfilled which saith, Abraham believed God, and it was imputed unto him for righteousness and he was called the Friend of God. Ye see then how that by works a man is justified, and not by faith only. (James 2:21–24)

What are we willing to give up to follow Christ? Why do we want what we want from God? Is it for the glory of God? Is love guiding our decision? Intimacy with our Lord is more than an experience. Intimacy is a lifestyle based on the Word of God. Intimacy with our Lord is exercising our God-given gift to produce fruit in our lives. I could not imagine what it was like to experience such intimacy with the Lord until I realize the difference between an experience and intimacy. By definition, an experience is an encounter or occurrence. It is the knowledge or mastery of an event or subject gained through involvement in or exposure to it. (google definition)

Unfortunately, it took me approximately seventeen years to really grasp these concepts. Through multiple trials and errors, I finally realized I couldn't do it in my own strength. I had to realize the power of God was the only way out of a repetitive cycle that had lasted for numerous years. The good news is that God's grace is sufficient and His mercy is everlasting as it is written. When I realized that I didn't want to experience one more day without God's power moving in my life, I cried out to the Lord with my whole heart for help. Well, HELP showed up in a mighty way. Thank You, Lord!

I decided wholly to submit my life to follow Christ. At this point of my journey, it really doesn't matter why it took me so long to realize that I had established a pattern of destruction when it came to all types of relationships, whether in my personal life, church, job, or friends. What mattered most to me is the fact that I had become someone that I really did not like myself. It was my rock bottom. I didn't feel good about myself nor my outcome. I had worn myself out trying to please everyone to the point that I was so heartbroken and weary. Yes, I was still reading the Word and speaking in tongues, but I was lost. I had multiple experiences with God's gift, but I was still denying the power thereof.

Without giving full disclosure, I remember that morning. Enough was enough! I knelt down on the side of my bed, crying out, "Abba Father in heaven, help me! I can't do this alone, Father. I give it all to you, Lord." It was so intense that morning. My cry was different than ever before I had made the decision to turn from my ways of trying to please others to pleasing God by surrendering all my mind, body, and soul to the Lord. I truly left everything on the altar that morning. That was the turning point for my entire life. I haven't looked back since. Thank you, Lord Almighty! I can truly say, "God is faithful." Hallelujah!

> From whence come wars and fighting among you? Come they not hence, even of your lusts that war in your members? Ye lust, and have not; ye kill, and desire to have, and cannot obtain: ye fight and war, yet ye have not, because ye ask not. Ye ask, and receive not, because ye ask amiss, that ye may consume it upon your lusts? Ye adulterers and adulteresses, know ye not that the friendship of the world is enmity with God? Whosoever therefore will be a friend of the world is the enemy of God. Do you think that the scripture saith in vain, the Spirit that dwelleth in us lusteth to envy? But he giveth more grace. Wherefore he saith, God resisteth the proud, but, giveth grace unto the humble. Submit yourselves therefore to God. Resist the devil, and he will flee from you. Draw nigh to God, and he will draw nigh to you. Cleanse your hands, ye sinners, and purify your hearts, ye double minded. Be afflicted, and mourn, and weep: let your laughter be turned to mourning, and your joy to heaviness. Humble yourselves in the sight of the Lord, and he shall lift you up. (James 4:1–10)

Thank you, Lord!

There is nothing like having power and not knowing what to do with it. After seventeen years of having received God's gift of the Holy Spirit, I had no clue that I was not submitted to the Holy Spirit. The Lord had mercy on me. It wasn't that I had not cried out to the Lord before to help me, but this cry was different. I no longer wanted to be a friend to the world. I didn't care what type of ridicule I would experience or who would walk out of my life. If I did not submit to the power of God, I somehow knew that the outcome would be devastating. More than anything, I just wanted to please God from that point on. I was tired of turning a deaf ear and blind eye to what I knew to be wrong. No more! I surrendered all that morning, and I have not looked back. Before that day, I could not have imagined this life that I now live in Christ. Hallelujah! Oh, what a change in my life. Thank You, Father in heaven. Thank you, Lord. The Holy Spirit is my helper!

> But ye shall receive power, after that the Holy Ghost is come upon you: and ye shall be witnesses unto me both in Jerusalem, and in all Judea, and in Samaria, and unto the uttermost part of the earth. (Acts 1:8)

Amen. Hallelujah!

October 9, 2019

Thank you, Father God, in heaven! There is none like you. Lord, I love you so much. I thank you for my husband, children, and entire family. Lord, I thank you for saving me. Your amazing grace, how sweet is the sound that saved a wretch like me. I once was lost, but now I am found. I was blind, but now I can see. Hallelujah! The storm is over now. Sweet Jesus!

2017 was definitely the year that God ignited the fire in my life. Thank You, Lord, for Your consuming fire. Hallelujah! I finally realized that I wasn't going to die. All my Father wanted from me is a true "yes, Lord," from my heart. It makes so much sense now. Up until that year, I realized that I wasn't trusting my Lord with every-thing. I realized that I was only giving Him part of me. I was saying one thing, but the fruit of my life was revealing my lack of faith. Father in heaven, thank You for loving me so that You chastised me. Thank You, Lord, for waiting on me. Thank You, Lord, for hearing my cry. Glory to God!

It is truly my prayer that you are being blessed by my testimony, and I am praying that I can explain how I am currently feeling and have been feeling since I truly laid down my life to follow Christ. God's consuming fire was ignited in me and all around me in the year of 2017, and it is still burning like new. My life is renewed daily. Hallelujah! All the glory belongs to God Almighty.

I remember when he told me, "No one will get the glory for what I am doing in your life but me." To this very day, I have given all the glory to God Almighty. As much as I love my husband, children, and entire family, no one comes before my Father in heaven. Thank You, Lord!

> And it came to pass, when ye heard the voice out of the mist of the darkness (for the moun-tain did burn with fire,) that ye came near unto me, even all the heads of your tribes, and your elders: And ye said, Behold the Lord our God hath shewed us his glory and his greatness, and we have heard his voice out of the mist of the fire; we have seen this day that God doth talk with man, and he liveth. (Deuteronomy 5:23–24)

> Now therefore why should we die for this great fire will consume us: if we hear the voice of the Lord our God anymore, then we shall die. For who is there of all flesh, that hath heard the voice of the living God speaking out of the midst of the fire, as we have and lived. Go thou near, and hear all that the Lord our God shall say; and speak thou unto thee; and we will hear it, and do

it. And the Lord heard the voice of your words, when ye spoke unto me; and the Lord said unto me, I have heard the voice of the words of this people, which they have spoken unto thee; they have well said all that they have spoken. O that there were such an heart in them, that they would fear me, and keep all my commandments always, that it might be well with them, and with their children forever. (Deuteronomy 5:25–29)

I truly love this passage in the scripture. God's Word is truly alive and well. This is Moses addressing the children of God and reminding them how God is faithful to His covenant people. Moses reflects on God's promises to those whom are obedient to His commandments. What is so intriguing about this passage is when the scripture is revealed and reminds the children of God, through Moses, that the Lord God Almighty had spoken. I can see the Father, Son, and Holy Spirit in this passage. The Triune God, I can see here. I can see His totality. I also can see myself here. Hallelujah! God is great! We, as believers, are not alone. God has not forsaken us. Remember, we are joint heirs with Christ. Remember, God's grace is sufficient. Remember, Jesus did not come to destroy the law, but to fulfil it. As believers, we are reconciled to God through Jesus Christ our Lord.

October 12, 2019

PAUSE. HALLELUJAH!

God Almighty, You are so awesome and so powerful. You are Lord! King of kings, Lord of lords, and Lord of host. Shouting in my spirit! "We have just witnessed another miracle." I tell you all that my body is tired, but my spirit is rejoicing this morning. Just as the beginning of this journey, I am elated at what the Lord has done.

For the past hour or two, I have been laying in my bed looking up at the ceiling watching the ceiling fan turn and thinking to myself, *Lord, You are so powerful.* All the glory belongs to God. I know, by now, you are thinking, "Why doesn't she just get to the point already?" Literally I am at awe and almost speechless.

What started off just being a usual morning ended up being another extraordinary moment in time. It was usual for my husband to call and wake me up before he would leave for work. He's always such a beautiful sight to wake up to. This morning, I could hardly keep my eyes open when our conversation started. I thought we were just going to greet each other, give God thanks, pray, and kiss the phone (lol) and then back to sleep for me. Nope, not this morning. My beloved husband started talking about patience and how the Lord blesses those who trust in Him and have patience to wait on Him. He looked at me and started telling me how much God loves us and favors us. He started reflecting on the most recent testimonies, just this, wherein the Lord had shown us favor with our family.

In the last two weeks, we have experienced God move in our finances, providing our daughter with a better job, our son coming home and returning back with his sister and job safely, healing in our family, and my husband settling in with his new position that was not so strenuous on him and our communication and not to mention how the Lord blessing me to be off on this Sunday as well.

You see, for the last eight years or more, the Lord has favored me to be off on Sundays. This privilege has been so beneficial in my growth in the Lord. Although I struggled with so much over the years, I believe my ability to come together with other believers and worship the Lord has strengthened my growth. The enemy knows that, and from time to time, he tries to disturb my peace by causing conflict among my coworkers. For this reason, I have to stay on my face and talk with the Lord. Just this week, God worked it out for me. One day at a time.

My husband often reminds me to trust God. I listen, and it all seems to work out in our favor. *Oh, okay, Marcia, stay focused and get to the meat of the blessing this morning.* Just like Moses encouraged the children of God before they entered the promised land, I could hear the Holy Spirit of the living God encourage me this morning. I thank God for the life that I now live in Christ. Just like my current job working among the mentally ill, life in Christ never ever gets dull. Life with Christ requires us, as believers, to stay focused on the kingdom. It requires us to love what we do. It requires us to give ourselves for the cause. Working among the mentally ill and living the life that I now live in Christ cause me to reflect over my life and see just how far God has brought us as well as how far He will take us only if we obey Him.

Yes, this morning, I am pausing just to reflect back on how God has delivered us time and time again, not only my family but also God's children especially those of the household of faith. Those that believe God and obey His Word are double blessed. There is no failing in God, our Lord. Hallelujah! There is no way that I can share my journey with you and not include the Word of God and testify of His goodness and mercy. This journey is a journey of thanksgiving. My prayer is that you are blessed and encouraged to follow Christ with us. We are family.

Okay okay okay! I have kept you in suspense long enough. Again, my husband called me this morning as usual, but he started getting very deep in conversation talking about how God rewards those who are patient and wait upon the Lord. I was so sleepy until he told me he was about to send me something via e-mail that he received at 12:00 a.m. I wondered what could that be. Suddenly, my mind started waking up. I sat up in bed. My eyes opened wider. There it was. I thought to myself, *Could it be?* My heart started racing. I started anticipating the e-mail. It seemed like minutes had gone by, but in fact it was only seconds before I received the e-mail. My husband's facial expression was so poised and relaxed while asking, "Baby, did it come through yet?" Lord knew what I needed in my husband. These last two and half years has taught me to trust God and have patience. I am truly a blessed woman. Oh, okay! Back to the e-mail. There it was, an e-mail received around 12:00 a.m. from NVC. Yes, just as I kept you at suspense, my husband had done the same to me. We are in it together. God did it again. Hallelujah!

The letter read, "Thank you for your interest in immigrating to the United States of America. The Department of State's NVC received your approved immigrant visa petition from US Citizenship and Immigration Services. NVC role is to ensure you are prepared for your immigrant visa interview at a US Embassy/Consulate General and to schedule your interview." Hallelujah! Yes yes yes! God had done it again. Right when our bodies were tired, when we felt like we could not stay awake or go an extra mile, God stepped in on time. God picked us up and carried us over a little further until we reached our destination. Thank You, Lord, for giving us hope that you haven't left or forsaken us. You, Father in heaven, shall complete what You started in Your children. It is our—my husband and I—hope God continue to keep and bless us all. Amen.

> Thy Word is a lamp unto our feet, and a light unto our path. (Psalm 119:105)

> Delight thyself also in the Lord, and He shall give thee the desires of thine heart. Commit thy way unto the Lord, trust also in Him; and he shall bring it to pass. (Psalm 37:4–5)

Thank You, Father in heaven, our Lord and Savior Jesus Christ, and Holy Spirt. There is none like You, Lord. Hallelujah! My soul rejoices. My life is changed by the power of the Holy Spirit. I take delight in Your Word, Lord. Glory to Your name. Lord, Your name is above all names. Hallelujah!

I am grateful for "I am." There is none like You, Lord. Your name is blessed. I give you glory, Father God, in heaven. Hallelujah! My soul rejoices. Lord, You keep doing great things for me. Thank You, Lord!

The Bible says, "And it shall come to pass, that "before they call, I will answer; and while they are yet speaking, I will hear" (Isaiah 65:24).

I am so grateful that You are in my life, Jesus. Thank You, Holy Spirit, for guiding me. Thank You, Father in heaven, for loving the world so much that You gave us Your beloved Son, Jesus Christ. Thank You, Father, for deciding to wrap Yourself up in human form and come down through generations just to die so that we would have an opportunity to live victoriously with Christ until life eternity with You, Father. Thank You for your anointing. Thank You for choosing Your children before we entered into this world. Now, we can live to the hope of our calling in Christ Jesus. Hallelujah! There is none like You, Lord. Everything I hope for is in You. It is a blessing to testify to Your love for me and my love for You, Lord.

Hallelujah! Thank You for allowing my daughter to call to testify to me last night and confirm to me through the man of God that knew neither of us by testifying that You, Father in heaven, hears my prayers by calling my name. Thank You for the Word, Lord. Amen.

October 22, 2019

Glory to God Almighty! I will bless the Lord at all times, and praises shall continuously be in my mouth. The Lord has been good to me. I will believe God's Word. I will not turn back. I will press forward in the name of Jesus. No matter what I see or hear that's contrary to the Word of God, I will not receive it. I will remain focused only on the Word of God. God's Word is the Truth. It is very powerful.

I am at a point in my life where there is absolutely no room for negativity or fear. I was just telling my husband that after I attended a revival tonight, my heart was only for the Word of God. I will not apologize if writings are sounding boring to you, the readers, because it is my choice to only focus on the positives and not the negative aspects of life. It is all about Jesus and what the Lord has done for us—all about Jesus, our wonderful Savior. No one shall get the glory but God Almighty for what He has done. Hallelujah! It is my desire to stay in the presence of the Lord. I pray that for both you and me. We can do this. No amount of money or fame can detour me from loving God. Do I still make mistakes along this journey? Yes, I do. But I am reminded of God's grace and mercy daily. I refuse to tolerate defeat, depression, intimidation, or fear any longer. No more by the power of the living God. Absolutely, no more!

My desire is to remain authentic with my relationship with the Lord Almighty and His creation. I refuse to live a lie. I know where my help comes from. When no one else was there for me, my Lord and Savior was there to pick me up. I owe my all and all to God Almighty, nobody but the Lord! It was nobody but the Lord that delivered me out of a horrible pit. Because that pit has no power over me now, I will continue to walk in the blessings of God until the day that Christ returns.

You do not have to remind me. I lean and depend on the Holy Spirit to lead me through this journey daily. We can do this together. We can make this choice together to pick up and cross and follow Jesus. Hallelujah! Lord, I thank You for changing me daily. Lord, I thank You for redeeming me. I believe You to save my entire family, and I believe You for miracles and blessings to be abundant in the body of Christ. Lord, I pray that You will give us grace to minister to one another in a way that Your power is demonstrated and souls will be added daily to your kingdom for Your name's sake. It is all about You, Father in heaven. Come nigh, my Lord Jesus Christ. Come nigh! Let us all be ready when You return, Lord. This I pray in the name of Jesus. Increase, Lord! Glory to God. Amen.

October 23, 2019

Thanking You, Lord for all You've done for me. Glory to Your name, for You are worthy, Lord. There is none like You. Jesus Christ, You are Lord over my life. This is the day that You have given me; and, Lord, I will rejoice and be glad in it. Fill me up with Your Spirit, Lord.

> O Lord our God, other lords beside thee have had dominion over us: but by thee only will we make mention of thy name. (Isaiah 26:13)

> Thou wilt keep him in perfect peace, whose mind is stayed on thee: because he trusteth in thee. Trust ye in the Lord for ever: for in the Lord JEHOVAH is everlasting strength. (Isaiah 26:3–4)

This Word has truly blessed me today. It is my prayer that you all are being blessed as well while we are experiencing this journey. Praise God for what He has already done. Thank You, thank You, thank You, Lord! Your Word is truly life to me, Lord. Thank You, Holy Spirit! Father God, in heaven, I pray that You would fill Your children up with Your anointing, for it is Your anointing that destroys the yoke.

> And it shall come to pass in that day, that his burden shall be taken away from off thy shoulder, and his yoke from off thy neck, and the yoke shall be destroyed because of the anointing. (Isaiah 10:27)

Have you ever been so inspired on the inside, but you literally did not exactly know how to put it all into words? This is how I feel right now. I am so grateful for our Lord and Savior. Just thinking about how awesome God is makes everything that I have experienced worth celebrating Him all day and every day. Hallelujah! I pray the power of God will continue to consume us as we journey together. I pray the Lord will bless your commitment to finish this journey with me. I pray the Lord Almighty bless me even more for allowing you all to share in my walk to destiny with Him. Yes, I am including myself in the blessing. Why not? We are all children of the Most High God. We are joint heirs to His inheritance (Son), only if we believe. I can hear the Spirit of God say, "Only trust God." I can hear my husband ask me, "Baby, who are you?" I used to wonder why my husband would ask me that so often, but the Lord was speaking through my husband to bring me into awareness and prompt me to seek the Lord's Word for answers. Yes, it worked. Hallelujah! Thank You, Jesus! Whatever we need is in the Word of God. Glory to God!

Waymaker, Miracle Worker, I believe God's Word. Lord, Your Word lives in me. Thank You, Jesus. Hallelujah! I remember when I started or made the decision to read the Bible. Nothing was making much sense to me, especially the Old Testament, which included Psalm and Proverbs. I had no idea of the blessing in just reading and trusting God to reveal who He is as my Lord and Redeemer and who I am in Christ. Thank You, Jesus. I had no idea what I was missing. Now, when I open up the Word of God, my sight is clearer, and my vision is improving daily. I pray that you too are experiencing a pure relationship with our Lord. Yes, He waited on us. Thank You, Lord, for Your mercy and grace. I owe You my life, Lord. Life with Christ is the best life. Glory!

THE INVITATION

I invite you! I challenge you, as you walk with me on this journey with Christ Jesus, to believe God. Yes, let's do this together. We got this. It is my prayer, by now, that you all have given your lives to the Lord and has made Jesus Christ your personal Lord and Savior just as I have committed and yielded my life to Him. Any other way, I believe, is a path of destruction. Jesus Christ is the Way to our Father in heaven. So if you haven't yet repented and confessed Jesus Christ as Lord and Savior, now is the time to pause and take this opportunity to do just that before it's too late. You are not alone. Amen.

> That if thou shalt confess with thy mouth the Lord Jesus, and shalt believe in thine heart that God hath raised him from the dead, thou shalt be saved. For with the mouth confession is made unto salvation. For the scripture saith, whosoever believeth on him shall not be ashamed. (Romans 9:9–11)

If you have been a late bloomer, it's okay. No better time than this time to answer the call of God. It doesn't matter how long it has taken. What matters most is that you, now, have chosen to surrender your all to Christ and let us allow our Lord and Savior to complete what He has started in us. Amen.

Thank You, Lord, for all You have done for me. I am determined to walk closer with Christ daily. Yesterday was such an exceptional expressing of God's love. This was not just the title of our Sunday school lesson, but God demonstrated His power once again in my life. It is my prayer that you are experiencing the same expression of God's love in your lives as we continue to embark on the journey. I believe without a shadow of doubt that this testament of thanksgiving that I am expressing, by journaling, has been designed by God. I have no doubt. Only by the Spirit of God that we get this opportunity to experience the demonstration of God's power while walking together with Him. He is our Good Shepherd, and He will take good care of His sheep. Hallelujah! I really should have taken the time yesterday to message you by journaling, but I was so overjoyed with the power of God that I just wanted to bathe in His presence. It was one of those days that even the bad looked good to me. Glory to God. Absolutely nothing could have gone wrong yesterday because I knew that I was in the presence of God. In His presence, we are protected. Hallelujah!

Father, I ask You now to allow me to experience that same level of your presence daily or higher. Take me higher in Your presence, Lord. It is Your presence that I find safety. All things are perfect in Your presence. Hallelujah!

The Bible says, "Thou wilt shew me the path of life: in thy presence is the fulness of joy; at the right hand there are pleasures for evermore" (Psalm 16:11).

I am shouting this morning. Glory to God! I truly pray that you can feel the presence of God. I cannot truly find the words to explain how elated I am every moment that God's presence is with me. Just now, I was about to stop writing because my sister was on her way to pick me up to take care of some personal business, but God! My plan, after finishing my last thought, was to close this journal up and open my Bible to read a scripture before I get in the shower. When I tell you that all I did was just open up my Bible and it landed on Psalm 16, believe me. I started to read toward the end of that chapter. The

Spirit of God led me straight to a scripture of confirmation. When I wrote my last passage, I was referencing to that scripture, but I did not know where it was in the Bible. I just had it in my heart. Look at God. Hallelujah! Shouting and praising Him. Listen, remember I spoke of yesterday's experience of God's presence. I never really told you exactly the testimonies that He gave me but just spoke of His presence. This is the same reason that I could not journal yesterday. I was and still am in the presence of God. The Holy Spirit will bring back to our memory God's Word. Hallelujah!

October 30, 2019

Help me, Holy Spirit. I need Thee, oh, Lord. Father God, in heaven, I am so thankful for another day that you have given me. You are so awesome, Lord. Hallelujah! Glory to Your name. Thank You, Jesus, for dying for us. Thank You, Jesus, for being the Way, Truth, and Life as it is written. Thank You, for saving us. If it had not been for You, Lord Almighty, where would we be? Thank You, Father God Almighty, for Your grace and mercy. Amen.

I am sitting here just thinking to myself on how good God is to His children. We, the children of God, are the most blessed generation. Just to think some of us will be still here standing when Jesus Christ returns. Oh, what a glorious day that will be. I am just thankful that we have time to get our lives in order. God has given us knowledge and grace to prepare for His second coming. Oh, happy day when Jesus comes. We are not bastard children. Jesus is coming soon. Everything has purpose in life. As life goes on, I find it easier to believe God's Word. It is my prayer that you have joined me as we walk this journey by faith for the glory of God. I am embracing every moment. I have purpose. Say it with me, "We have purpose in Jesus's name." HALLELUJAH!

There is so much I can say that I am not saying as we journey together with Christ. The Word is so true. When we delight ourselves in the Lord, He will give us the desires of our hearts as it is written. God's Word is the truth. I can honestly say I believe God at His Word more today than I have ever. The Lord is about demonstrating

His power. Hallelujah! Even when it comes to my husband and the immigration case, the Lord is performing miracles even as I journey with you. I believe, in the near future, we will get the opportunity to truly tell our testimony, but in the meanwhile, we will continue to offer up praise unto the Lord. Glory to God!

It is a choice to believe God. All we have to do is just simply believe God. Just believe. Even if we do not see and feel, just believe God. We owe Him that. Why can we not just believe God at His Word? If it be any unbelief found in us, help our unbelief Lord. The world will be a better place if we only believe God's Word not sometimes but all the time. It is my prayer that we journey together and believe our Lord to finish or complete what He has started in us for His glory. We can do this not because of what He can do for us, but because of what He has already done for us in giving Himself to die for us that we may have life more abundantly. Are you ready?

November 4, 2019

Thank You, Father in heaven! There is none like you. Hallelujah! Glory to Your holy name, Lord Jehovah. There is power in the name of Jesus. There is hope and deliverance in the name of Jesus. Come nigh, our Lord. Come nigh! Make us a ready people to received You as You return, for You, Lord Jesus, is surely to come. Help us, Lord!

> Therefore shall a man leave his father and his mother, and shall cleave unto his wife: and they shall be one flesh. (Genesis 2:24)

> And said, For this cause shall a man leave his father and mother, and shall cleave to his wife: and they twain shall be one flesh? (Matthew 19:5)

> Wherefore they are no more twain, but one flesh. What therefore God hath joined together let no man put asunder. (Matthew 19:6)

I feel led by the Spirit of God this morning to make reference to and speak on this subject of marriage. As you know, up until this moment, I have not really spoken on this subject. I can feel the presence of God, and He is about doing great miracles our lives. Amen.

I do not know you personally, but I can feel you spiritually, my brothers and sisters, in Christ. Are you ready for God to perform a miracle in our lives? We are in this together. Do you believe the Word of God? I believe God. Hallelujah! I can see my harvest. Just this morning, I have asked my Lord to prepare me for the upcoming harvest. It's coming soon, saints. I am not just talking about our desires that we have before the Lord. I am talking about Jesus Himself. Did you not know that He is coming back for His bride, the church? Hallelujah! Are we ready?

November is the month that the masses celebrate Thanksgiving; however, if we just learn to be thankful unto our Lord and Savior at all times. Lately, I have been feeling the push to just simply tell the Lord, "Thank You, Lord," at all times. Thank You. Thank You. Thank You, Lord! Hallelujah! This is what this journey is about. Let's give God the glory for what He has already done. Did you hear me? It's already done. Hallelujah! Just believe and receive the blessing of God! Just to know the Lord is a blessing.

LOVE IS THE GREATEST

This journey that I have embarked on since 2017 has been simply amazing. Submitting myself to the will of God has been the absolute best thing that I could have ever done. It was my biggest investment, or shall I say, the biggest investment that I could have ever made in life. No amount of money could compare to it. My prayer today is that the Lord will give me the exact words to say to you that would explain my love for Him and His love for me. No other love can compare to the love that I feel in my heart for my Lord and Savior, my Father in heaven, my Redeemer, my present Help in a time of trouble, my Healer. Falling in love with Jesus was the best thing I ever could have done. Hallelujah!

It is so amazing just to experience the love that our Father in heaven has for us. There is no respect of persons. I thank God for the life that I now live in Christ Jesus. Please do not allow anyone to tell you anything different than the fact that our Father in heaven loves us. This love is not contingent on what He can do for us or what we can do for Him. It's all about what He has already done for us because He is LOVE. Did you hear me? God is love. When we truly experience this love, then we will know true love, and everything about us will become new. Hallelujah!

True love will make you forget past hurts and disappointments. I literally cannot remember the pain of my past. Forgiveness comes easy with true love. Not many people get the opportunity to experience it, but that does not mean that it was not available to them at all times. There is absolutely no way to experience true love without submitting our all to Christ and receiving love from our Father in heaven. God is love, remember! Say it with me, "God is Love!" Amen. Anything or anyone outside of "God is Love" is not of God. The contrast of love is hate. There is no in between. The contrast of good is evil. The contrast of truth is lie. Do I need to go on?

"For God so loved the world, that he gave his only begotten Son, that whosoever believeth in him should not perish, but have everlasting life" (John 3:16).

No one else or nothing else can take ownership of what is not theirs to give. Okay, ask me, "What are you saying, Marcia?" What I am saying is simple and powerful. The only way to know love is through Jesus Christ, our Lord and Savior. There is no other way to know God Almighty. The only way to the Father is through His Son. When we have seen His Son, we have seen the Father as it is written. This is LOVE. Hallelujah! This is so simple and powerful that most people miss it or have a delayed reaction. There are some things we do not have to endure if we only know and experience the true essence of God's love.

Today, it is on my heart to speak on marriage and love. God is about to do it. It is all about God and our relationship with Him first. How can I speak on our marriage without acknowledging our relationship with our Lord first? There would be no marriage without LOVE. Glory to God. Ask me how I know? Because, I tried it, and I learned it the hard way. I thank God for His grace and mercy through it all. That's another testimony for another time. This life that I now live is truly in Christ. Christ first. Amen.

Over the weekend, I was hanging out with one of my sisters. We came across a doctor from my job that had spoken words of wisdom in my life. Every time I see Dr. W., she would remind me of those words, and I would always be encouraged by them. Dr. W. is now eighty years old and still looks amazing. She told me and my sister that she was still working full time and had two jobs now. Wow! I remember a couple of years ago, I came across Dr. W. in the hallway of the hospital, and we chatted. I asked her, "What is your secret for looking so amazing?" She told me to live in the present, forget about past hurts, always forgive, eat right, take care of my body, and be joyful. What really moved me was when she told me to let the past go and move forward. I felt a release. It was that same year that I totally surrendered and committed my life to Christ—mind, body, and soul. I call the year of 2017 my birthing year. Hallelujah! It was the same year that I got baptized in Jesus's name unapologetic and asked that the power of the Holy Spirit overshadow me and fill me. That was the year that yokes were destroyed and chains broken and healed from my past failures and brokenness. My future became brighter, and most of all, LOVE lifted me. Hallelujah!

2017 was my year of transformation. It was the year that Christ set my life on the right path to righteousness. The Lord heard my cry and answered my call. I said yes to His will for my life. Hallelujah! It was the year the Lord started answering the desires of my heart. Yes yes yes! I started reaping the harvest in the same year, keeping my mind on Christ and delighting myself in the Lord. In other words, I didn't know my desires until I truly received LOVE. It starts and ends with our Lord Almighty. You don't have to ever put it down or lay it to the side to appease yourself or anyone else. No compromising LOVE. LOVE comes first. Without LOVE, we will fail. If we do not love, we do not know God. Everything is connected by LOVE in the kingdom of God. This is truly a love affair. Although my vision of love had grown dim over the years, the Lord restored my vision of LOVE in the same year that I cried out from my heart, "Lord, help me!" Out of the heart, the mouth speaks. Our way is limited, but God's way is eternal. LOVE is eternal. It has to be done God's way. There is no other way to enter into the presence of God. I could not have imagined this kind of LOVE. I am grateful. I am humbled. I am blessed. Thank You, Lord!

Let's praise God for what HE has done. Thank You, Lord, for Your love. We receive Your love. Freely, we received, and freely, we will give, Lord. No more fear. No more anxiety. No more lack. Father in heaven, we are open to receive Your gifts of the Holy Spirit. Father, we are ready to receive Your answers to our heart's desires. Thank You, Lord. Hallelujah!

I do not know about you, but I feel a great breakthrough. I woke up this morning and spent time in prayer, and the Lord put marriage on my heart. The Lord has already done it. Do you believe it? Not only do I believe God, but also this life that I now live in Christ is well received. I receive Your love, God, in my marriage, my family, my finances, and health. Thank You, Lord! I am so glad about it, Lord, for the life that You have allowed me to experience with You. Father God, I receive the husband that You have given me. Thank You, Lord, for the love that he has for me, a million miles away, but LOVE has no distance. Hallelujah! I receive, Lord. Amen.

Yes, Lord, I am now ready to receive my husband home. Hubby, come home in Jesus's name. It has been two and a half years since my husband has located me and still holding strong anticipating his homecoming. I feel it. It has been established and approved by God. Hallelujah! I feel a release in the spiritual realm. I receive the blessing. I am ready for the manifestation of Your promise, Lord. Thank You for teaching me, Holy Spirit. Thank You for putting in Your power, Lord. There is none like You, Lord. My beloved husband, come home now in Jesus's name.

Africa, it's time to release my husband to join his wife. It's time for my husband to leave his mother and father and become one with his wife. Thank You, Father in heaven, for Your Word today. It is time. Hallelujah! Thank You, Father in heaven, for preparing me to receive Your gift of LOVE as well as my heart's desire for a husband that loves his wife as Christ loves the church. It's Your doing, Lord, and we honor You in all our ways. Father, Your word says the gates of hell shall not prevail against the church. Also, what therefore You, Father, hath join together, let no man put asunder as it is written. I declare Your Word as our portion in Jesus's name. We receive. Hallelujah! Your daughter and son are ready, and Your Word has been established as a foundation of our marriage, and I am ready to receive my husband home in Jesus's name. Amen.

I AM READY

Thank You, Lord. Glory to Your, holy name, Jehovah. Hallelujah! There is none like You, Lord. Lord, You keep doing great things for me. Great grace, Lord. I hear You, Lord. Here I am. I am available Lord to You. Amen.

Saints of God, here I am sitting at my kitchen table reflecting on how great is our God. I hope, by now, we are walking together with Jesus. Are you ready for more? Say it with me, "Great grace Lord. Great grace." Hallelujah!

Just a couple of hours ago, I was praising God, and this song "I still Have Joy" by the Spiritualettes blessed me. I hope this is your testimony as well. We are blessed. If you have made it this far in your reading as we journey with Christ, you are blessed as well. Say it, "I am blessed."

My husband always asks me, "Baby, do you know who you are?" I remember a dream that I had with the Lord asking me the same question, "Who are you?" I had no idea at that time what I was hearing or why He asked me that. Now, my husband always gives the same reference in asking me, "Baby, do you know who you are?" I remember right before I woke up from the dream, it was the Word of God that was the link between me and my Lord. I literally held my Bible in my hand, while the Lord held my hand. When I woke up, my right fist was clenched with my prayer tallit. So amazing is our Lord. Hallelujah! I knew in my heart that in order for me to know who I am, I had to pick up the Word of God and study more and pray to our Father to reveal to me who I am in Christ through His Word. Hallelujah!

I am ready, Lord. Give me great grace, Lord. Amen. There is none like You. Saints, we need the Word of God to find out who we are. Saints, we need prayer for strength. Saints, we need to praise and worship our Lord. It's all a part of who we are in Christ. Hallelujah! Even every time when I go to speak on all the blessings that I have received over these last two years alone, I cannot seem to get past giving the Lord Almighty the glory for all He has done. My delight is in the Lord. I am so thankful for what He has done in my life. My joy is in the Lord. I still have joy. I still have God. God will never fail me because my delight is in the Lord. I pray that this is your testimony as well, not because of our possessions. This should be our testimony because God is God. Hallelujah! He is the Lord of lords, King of kings, and Lord of hosts. I am ready, Lord, for great grace. Hallelujah! I am ready. Destiny awaits me. Say it with me, "Destiny awaits me." Yes, we can do this by the Spirit of God. Amen.

Delight thyself also in the Lord; and he shall give thee the desires of thine heart. Commit thy way unto the Lord; trust also in him; and he shall bring it to pass" (Psalm 37:4–5).

November 8, 2019

Good morning, Holy Spirit. Glory to God Almighty. Thank You, Lord God, for another opportunity to wake up and praise You this morning. I am so grateful for all that You have done in my life. I choose to delight myself in You, Lord. Use me to Your will from today. Father in heaven, I love You. I thank You for life, to breathe, to walk, to talk, and now to live the life that I now live in Christ. Hallelujah! Father, I give you my all and all. Nobody like You, Lord. Amen.

Saints of God, it is my heart's desire to grow deeper in the things of God. Nothing else matters than to please our Father in heaven. I am overjoyed this morning. Thank You, Jesus. I believe by faith that Jesus is Lord. Hallelujah! Nothing can turn me around. This joy that I have, the world did not give it to me, and the world cannot take it away. Hallelujah! Yes, I am ready, Lord. I am ready for my promise, Lord. Those mighty men (Abraham, Isaac, and Jacob) are my inspiration all the way to my Lord and Savior, Jesus Christ. Glory to God! I declare that this day is a day of victory through Christ Jesus. I command this day, by the power of the living God, to produce harvest in my season. This is my season. Thank You, Lord, for all the love that You have shown Your children. Your Word tells us that Your sheep knows Your voice. I hear You, Lord. Let Your consuming fire go before my family today. Lord, everything that would attempt to separate us from You, destroy it by fire now in Jesus name. Victory belongs to Jesus. We have the victory through Christ Jesus. Amen.

November 14, 2019

Thank You, Father in heaven, for Your Son Jesus Christ our Lord. Thank You, Father, for Your Love. Thank You for being love. Thank You for the comfort of Your Holy Spirit. Here I am, Lord. As I bow before You this morning, I give thanks. You have given me another opportunity to be better. Hallelujah! Better days are ahead of me, my family, and the body of Christ. You have not forsaken us, Lord. You are precious to me. For that, I am grateful. Oh, how I am so grateful! It is your power that sustains me, my family, and the body of Christ. Lord, I love You. Lord, I trust You. Lord, I believe in You. Lord, I am ready. Hallelujah! Come nigh, my Lord. Come nigh! Holy is Thy name. You are King of kings, Lord of lords, and Lord of hosts. Thank You, Father. Thank You for knowing Your children. I love You so much, Lord, my Father, and Savior Jesus Christ. I am walking in expectation of Your Word today, all day, every day, and all my life for eternity in the name of Jesus. I walk in victory. I walk in favor because of You, Lord. It is nobody but You, Lord, that I will serve for the rest of my life. I plead the precious blood of Jesus over and around my entire family as bloodline to protect us from every fiery dart of the wicked. I put on the whole armor of God to stand against the wiles of the enemy in Jesus name. Amen.

Thank You, Lord. Hallelujah! You deserve the glory and the honor, Lord. I worship You, my Lord. You are worthy to be praised. Hallelujah! I need You, Lord. Father, You are my first love. I believe Your Word. Thank You, Father, for being lord over my life as well as lord over my family.

Saints of God, the Word of God is true. I am convinced that when we decide to submit to the will of God, there is nothing that God won't do for us. He will show up every time. Once again, my Lord showed up to fight my battle. The battle is won. Lord, You are our battle-ax. Hallelujah!

TESTIMONY

After a week of going back and forth with my job in regard to adding my husband to my medical insurance in preparation for him to come home to his wife, both me and my lawyer concluded that I should address the no's that the office kept giving me. All I was hearing was, "No no no," but the office was not able to effectively explain the reasons behind the no's. It was so frustrating to hear. Here we were at the last stage of our immigration process, and all I could hear was, "No no no." I did not even realize, at the time, the answer to our question was right there in my hand. It was the letter that I had just received a day before from the human resource personnel. It was not what the letter said that made all the difference. It was what the letter did not include. After scanning and sending the letter to my lawyer's office, I received an e-mail in response. In this e-mail, my lawyer's office pointed out the absence of the question that was specifically asked to address. The letter was so vague that it prompted questions by my lawyer's office and myself. In the midst of going back and forth with my lawyer's office in regard to this matter, I received a call from one of my sisters. I decided to share with her the dilemma. It did not take her long to tell me to get up, put on some clothes, and go back up to my job to look into these matters until I received the answers that I needed. So I did just that and some. I got up, put on my clothes, and called several family members to stand with me in prayer. I prayed the Lord's Prayer and asked the Lord to send His holy angels before me. I asked the Lord to let everything go according to His will and for it to be simple, powerful, and effective. Guess what? My Father answered our prayers immediately. No was not an option. The Lord of host had given us favor with Him and man. God's answer, for His children, is "yes and amen," Hallelujah!

Father, you keep making a way. Saints of God, only trust God. When man say no, God says yes when it is His will for our lives. The Lord had done above all that I could ask or think. When I left my job's human resource department, I left with a certificate of healthcare coverage for my husband. "I am" has spoken. Hallelujah! I believe God to bring my husband soon. What a mighty God we serve. Amen.

I declare that this is my harvest season for the glory of God! Hallelujah! This battle belongs to the Lord. Glory to God! While walking together, on this journey, it is my prayer that you all are being blessed as well. It is God Almighty's Will to bless His children. It is the Lord's Will that a man leave his mother and father and cleave to His wife. If God said it, it must come to pass. The Lord is a merciful Father. It takes consistency, persistence, patience, and prayer to walk this journey with Christ. It takes love, forgiveness, and mercy on this journey. It is my prayer that you all are motivated today to keep on walking with Christ because He is Lord over us, His children. Hallelujah!

November 28, 2019

Hallelujah! Glory to God Almighty! I'm singing

I'm reaching the harvest God has promised me
taking back what the devil stole from me
I rejoice today for I shall recover it all.

Hallelujah!

The Lord, God Almighty, is so awesome. He just keeps on doing great things for his children. I know that the Lord loves us all, but what I truly appreciate and love about our Father is His amazing ability to make us feel like we are the only one in the room. When it is our season for harvest, the Lord really is glorified through our lives. It is all about the glory of God being revealed through the lives of His children. Hallelujah! I can see clearly now. The rain is gone. I feel like singing. I feel like the victory is won. The Lord shall recover all. Because, we belong to Him, we shall recover all. Hallelujah! The presence of the Lord is here. I feel him in the atmosphere. Glory!

Over the last few days, there were so many challenges that both me and my husband and I were faced with. But Jesus Christ is real in our soul. One day we will be able to share with you all the challenges we endured, but I have decided that this is not the time. I just want to spend this journey testifying of God's goodness and mercy. Hallelujah! I even felt like writing in another color of ink today because I can feel a great shift. Hallelujah! I'm ready, Lord! Amen.

November 30, 2019

Hallelujah! Glory to God. Lord, You are worthy to be praised. There is no one like You, Lord. I am thankful for Your grace, Lord Almighty. I choose not to give the enemy a platform today or no other day for the rest of my life. I know who I am in Christ Jesus. No matter what the test, Lord, You have given me exactly what I need to pass. So I choose to smile and rejoice today. Hallelujah! What others do that is contrary to Your holy Word is their choice. As for me, I choose to continue to obey Your Word and live the life, in Christ, that I am learning about. Yes, every day is truly another opportunity to bless Your holy name, Jehovah. Hallelujah! Thank You, Father. I am so thankful that I can just simply be me. The world no longer has a hold on me. The world no longer dictates my emotions. Thank You, Lord. Just as the world has a right to reject me. I have the same right to reject the world now. Lord, everything that I possess and everything that You created me, for I give it all back to You. Father, let You light be glorified through my life and decisions. My answer today and every day is "yes, Lord"—yes to your will and yes to your way, Lord. I am ready. I will stay ready. I decree that no matter what the test, I will bless Your holy name, Lord. Father, I bless Your name, Lord, today and forevermore. Thank You, Lord!

December 5, 2019

Hallelujah! Glory to Your name, Lord. I will bless God at all time and praises shall continuously be in my mouth. Oh, magnify the Lord with me for He is great and worthy to be praised.

Well, Lord, You have done it again. You have answered our prayers once again. Thank You, Lord, for allowing our documents to arrive to Ghana safely in the hands of my precious husband. Thank You, Lord, for Your confirmation that all is well. Thank You, Lord, for allowing our civil documents to be scanned by our lawyer and sent to the embassy in Ghana. Hallelujah! Thank You, Jesus. Thank You, Father, for the power of the Holy Ghost. Thank You, Father, for Your holy angels that surround our family. Thank You, Father God, in heaven for healing our precious daughter and son. Thank You, Lord, that all is well with our family. Father, we owe our all to You. No weapon formed against my family shall prosper in Jesus name. Hallelujah!

Saints of God, I am determined to finish this journey that has been set before me. With the continued help of our Comforter and guidance of the spirit of Truth, all things are possible through Christ. It is my prayer that you all too are experiencing such breakthroughs and miracles that can only be contributed to the life that we now live through Christ Jesus.

December 7, 2019

Thank You, Lord. There is none like You, Lord. I am so grateful to call You Father. Hallelujah! Glory to Your name. I am truly in love with You, Lord.

Saints of God, I am so grateful to know Jesus. It is my prayer that you too are experiencing such amazing love liken to that of our Father. God is love. I am experiencing such amazing love from heaven above. No amount of money or riches can compare. Listen, I truly thank God Almighty for my beloved husband, our children, family, and all the blessings that He has blessed us with on this side of heaven. Everything matters with the Lord, from the smallest to the greatest, for it all comes from heaven above. However, nothing compares to the intimacy and love that we experience through the life that we now live in Christ Jesus. There is NO EXCUSE because this LOVE has been here from the beginning and will be through the end awaiting Christ's return no matter the tests before us. God is Love. God's love cannot be measured or contained. I should have received this LOVE a long time ago. All I had to do is surrender my all to GOD's LOVE and receive it. Wow! God's love is multidimensional. Just as I am journaling this experience with you, His love is overshadowing me. The spirit of Truth is here. The absolute best thing I could have done in my life in 2017 was to abandon my will for the will of God to be done in my life. I look forward to life eternally with Christ, but I am thanking God Almighty for this life as well that He has graced us with. Hallelujah! I invite you to do the same and join me on the happy road to our destiny, looking for Christ's return but experiencing the benefits to being the King of king's children now in the Lord. Hallelujah!

December 13, 2019

Hallelujah! Glory to Your name, Father God, in heaven. I will always praise You, Lord. Thank You, Jesus. There is none like You, Lord. Jehovah is Your name. Amen.

Saints of God, this morning is like no other morning that I have experienced before. There is no way to describe how I feel at this particular moment. The first word to come to my mind is "SOLEMN." I hope I just spelled it right. Oh well, I will look it up later. I shake my head as I write this letter to you this morning. You know, sometimes you just know. This morning is one of those moments that you just know what you know, or shall I rephrase that to say, "I just know that I know by the Spirit of God."

I just woke up from the most powerful dream. Well, I suppose it was a dream. All I can tell you is that when one has had an encounter with the Lord God Almighty, you just know what you know. There is no debate to knowing God. Hallelujah! My body feels limp. My back and hands feel like someone has poured hot anointing oil over me. I feel the lines gathering in my face as I ask the Lord, "Lord, is this what grace feels like?" I feel like crying and dancing at the exact same time. Is the worship, Lord? This experience got to be the true essence of what worshipping Jehovah in spirit and truth feels like. It's nothing like I have experienced before. We know about the raising of hands to reference our Lord and Savior, but true worship cannot be seen. Hallelujah! True worship has to be experienced. Glory to God. "How do you know, Marcia?" Well, thank you for asking. I know only by the spirit of the Lord. Amen. It is my prayer that someone is getting this, or shall I say, "I pray that someone is experiencing this moment with me as I am experiencing it with the Lord and Savior." Hallelujah!

It's only by the spirit of the Lord that I am sharing this with you. The Lord has given me liberty to do just that, and I am happy to do it. It's all about knowing this morning. You just know saints. All have not been told. Saints, we serve a mighty God of battle. He is our battle-ax. Jehovah is his name. He is the God of heaven and earth. He is Lord over all flesh. He is our Creator. He is the Beginning and the End. He is the Alpha and Omega. There is none like Him. He is the Decision-Maker. He is our Waymaker. Hallelujah!

Y'all! Yes, I said y'all. Lol. I am from the country, and I am gaining strength in my body as I write to you, though I'm still shaking my head from side to side, just thinking about, *Oh, how great is our Lord God!* Hallelujah! So please let me have a moment now and address y'all as y'all. Y'all, God is great and greatly to be praised. Amen.

I know that it is now 6:15 a.m. because my alarm has just notified me. I started writing at 5:45 a.m. I have yet to share the dream because I have been in awe at how powerful the experience is upon waking up. Pure worship, only God knows. Glory to God!

I also feel led to share another experience with you all from a few years ago along with this current worship experience from this morning. I heard the spirit of the Lord say, immediately, "This is the way." Hallelujah! Saints of God, you have heard it as I have this morning. This was the theme of my experience just a few years ago that I am led to share this morning. I hope you will be blessed as well.

I remember, a few years ago, I was at a crossroad on my way to church. I was between churches at the time. The Lord was leading me in another direction, but the decision wasn't that clear to me. So this particular morning, I was running late to church on Easter. If I am not mistaken, it was the Easter of 2017. Yes, 2017 was when I was at a crossroad in life. Though there are many crossroads in our lives, this one was peculiar. I just knew it. There I was headed out of the city, going south and almost stopping in the middle of the highway because I heard the Spirit of God, I believe, tell me to turn around and go in the opposite direction. I didn't know where I was going, but I knew that it had to be the voice of the Lord because I had been feeling a nudge all morning that I was ignoring.

There I was driving in the opposite direction following what I believed to be the voice of the Lord. I didn't know where or why, but it was all about obedience and knowing. Yes, you'll know. Hallelujah! I might have driven about two miles; and there it was, this church that sat off to itself, grass not mowed and with only three cars in the parking lot, and it was on Easter. I found myself driving past the church asking the Lord, "Lord, are you sure?" I got down about two blocks, and the spirit of the Lord said, "Go back!" I turned around and obeyed God. Thank You, Lord, that by the time I went back, there was a woman outside with her children who was preparing to go inside to service. I got out of the car, introduced myself, and went in with them so that I did not have to go in alone. Thank You, Jesus. I didn't know anyone there and found myself waiting on the Word of God. I knew the Word was also there waiting on me. Hallelujah!

Saints of God, please hear me. If we be in Christ, we are not alone. We are one with our Father through our Lord Jesus Christ, and He has given us His Holy Spirit to ensure the fellowship with our Lord. The only way to the Father is through His Son. There is no other way. Our whole life is prophetic. The Word of God is prophecy, and our Lord knows the plan that He has for us. All we have to do is trust and obey His Word. Saints of God, please hear me. We are a team! We are reconciled through Christ Jesus. Hallelujah!

Oh, did I mention that I got to church late but not denied the Word of God? Just as soon as I sat down, the preacher was getting up to deliver God's Word that had been prepared. Thank You, Jesus. Hallelujah! God is so intentional and amazing. I am trying my best to share with you this morning, as I am experiencing the presence and blessings of the Lord. All have not been told. Please, hear me. You are experiencing this moment as I am experiencing it by the grace of God. I know it might sound repetitive that I am saying, "Listen, saints," but it's only because I am trying to contain myself enough to explain to you how our destiny has already been settled in heaven. All we have to do is submit our will over to God's will no matter how it looks or feels for the glory of God to be revealed to us and through our lives. We must have a conversation with our Lord. Our relationship with our Lord is not one-sided. The Lord is a gentleman. He doesn't just speak to us. He listens to our desires as well. God hears us. Are you glad about it? I know that I have not got to the dream this morning. Please be patient. You will understand just why I am reflecting back to 2017, on that Easter morning, in just a few. The Holy Spirit is revealing to me as I am writing to you so we all get to experience this precious moment of blessing together.

Thank You, Lord, for reminding me of Your spoken word. Hallelujah! Glory to Your name, Lord Jehovah!

Saints of God, the Word of the Lord for that that Sunday was, "It is finished!" I am sitting here reflecting on the notes from that Sunday. The man of God talked about staying the course and not giving up even when you believe you have made the wrong turn or decision. He encouraged the believers to keep trying and believing God Almighty to complete what He has started in us. "Hang in there," was his message to the saints. It was the Sunday that Christians celebrate the resurrection of Christ Jesus. To be exact, it was April 16, 2017, according to my journal. I still have the program from that Sunday. I receive this word even now! Thank You, Holy Spirit, for reminding me, through the life of Christ, that we must finish the course because our case has already been settled in heaven.

Hallelujah! Yes, "it is finished" was the message. The name of that ministry was just as powerful. The name "God's Way Fellowship" reminded me that "it" has to be God's way. Amen.

What has God placed on our hearts to do? What is our heart's desire? We are reminded by God's daily bread that we have purpose through the life of our Lord and Savior. While on earth, all Jesus wanted to do is our Father's will, and He has done exactly that. He is our Redeemer. We too through Christ have to do our Father's will for our lives. We have to do it Jehovah's way. Hallelujah! Yes, "it is finished" tells us that we are victorious through Christ. Lord Jehovah will fight our every battle. Peace be with us. Amen.

I believe the dream that the Lord allowed me to experience this morning was to open my eyes up spiritually to what actually took place physically on April 16, 2017, Resurrection Sunday. You see, I was at a crossroad in making a decision, but I did not really grasp that the decision had already been settled in heaven. All I did at the crossroad was obey what I believed was God's voice and waiting on the Lord to give more direction. Initially, I was going to visit my family's church, but I knew at the time that it really was not settled in my heart that particular Sunday to go there. Me turning around and driving the opposite direction did not have anything to do with me not wanting to fellowship with family, but it had everything to do with wanting to obey the voice of the Lord (even if I did not know where the Spirit of God was leading me to). I had to move by faith. Hallelujah!

What I remember about the dream this morning, about three hours ago, was my body being dipped into a large tank of anointing oil. My eyes were open the whole time that I was there. I was about to see everything that was around me. I felt protected and at peace. From there, I found myself at the table in the presence of the heavenly court or counselors. I knew by the Spirit of God that a decision was being settled in heaven on my behalf. The oil represented the grace of God to do physically what has already been settle in heaven spiritually by Jehovah's court. This is December 13, 2019. Glory to God!

About three hours ago in December 13, our Lord Jehovah reminded me in a dream that my case has been settled, and now, I am about to see the physical manifestation of what has been settled in court. I do not know all (my case) details, but what I do know is that my case is settled in the heavenly court with the decision in my favor by our Father in heaven, Lord Jehovah. Hallelujah!

The last thing that I remember was sitting in front of our Righteous Judge with councilmen (elders) on each side. I was thinking in my heart, *Jehovah is His name.*

Then, right in front of me, the Righteous Judge spoke, "Are you ready?"

I said, "I am ready, Lord."

"Jehovah is my name," he spoke to me.

I cannot describe how I truly felt at that moment—totally at awe—but this does not even come close to describing how I feel. Hallelujah! Thank You, Lord God, for allowing me to see your heavenly court when our case comes before you and reminding us that "it is finished" on the day that the church celebrates our Lord and Savior, Jesus Christ—resurrection. Jehovah is Your name Lord. Hallelujah! Glory to God. Thank You, Lord, for grace. Amen.

IT'S ALREADY DONE

Thank You, Lord, for not only a brand new day but also a new season in my life. I take joy any day over pain that a life of sin produces. I thank You, Lord, for salvation. Your joy, Lord Almighty, is truly my strength. Thank You for joy. Hallelujah! Thank you. Thank you. Thank You, Jesus! Glory to God. I lift Your name up, Lord. Your name is above every name. There is power in the name of Jesus. Thank You, Father, for a renewed mind. Thank You for mind to praise You at all times. There is none like You, Lord. Hallelujah!

Saints of God, Jesus is truly the reason for this season that we are experiencing. It is my prayer that your life has a new sound to it as we continue to experience the blessings of the Lord daily. It is good to know the Lord Jesus no matter where we find ourselves at in life. Because we are in Christ Jesus, nothing can separate us from the love of God. God is love. We have that same love resonating on the inside of us. Are you glad about it? I am glad about it. Hallelujah! My mom used to sing "He'll make a way somehow. Yes, He will!" Amen.

It is already done. Hallelujah! Receive the Word of the Lord along with me. It is the will of our Father in heaven that we all prosper even as our soul prospers. Glory to God! As believers of Christ, we have to continue to study, learn, and know the language of our Father in heaven to be able to effectively communicate with Him. How are we going to know what is on His heart if we do not know how to speak His language? How? Remember, we are in this together. We have to remember that we are a team. We come as a package mended together for delivery. There is no separating us from the love of our God. His name is Emmanuel. Hallelujah! Who can stand against our Lord?

Our Lord Jehovah is a righteous judge. We must remember that our case has already been settled in the heavenly court. We must remember the goodness of the Lord if we expect to prosper. This is our season. We dare not to forget who did it. What is His name? Emmanuel (the Lord with us). The Lord is present. I decree over lives that we are victorious through Christ Jesus. I pray the power of God will fill us today and every day and that His will be done in our lives. I pray we never forget how Jehovah has delivered us from the enemy. I declare over our lives that we want look or turn back lest we fall. Help us, Holy Spirit. I decree that no weapon formed against us shall prosper in Jesus name. Amen.

December 21, 2019

Good morning, Holy Spirit! There is none like You, Lord. I am grateful that You, Father God, is leading and guiding me through this path of righteousness for Your name's sake. Jehovah is Your name. Thank You for the power of Your Spirit. Thank You, Jesus Christ. I thank You because there is no separation in You, Lord. Hallelujah! You are my Peace. You are my Joy. You are my Healer. Father, You are my all and all. I love You so much, Lord. Glory to Your holy name. I will continue to trust the process. Thank You for renewing my mind daily by Your Word, Lord. Hallelujah!

Father God in heaven, I thank You for my life in Christ Jesus. I thank You that I get the opportunity to learn of You each day. To get to know You, Lord, is to get to know who You have created me to be. I thank You that I get the opportunity to walk closer with You on this side of heaven. I thank You, Father, for saving my soul. I thank You for every trial or test that You brought me through. I thank You for fighting my battles and showing me, through Your Spirit, how to war in the spirit. Thank You, Lord. Hallelujah! No matter how my flesh feels at times, I thank You for giving me the power to deny it. Thank You, Lord, that my soul is happy. I rejoice in the Lord. Thank You for being my strength. Thank You for using my eyes, hands, ears, mouth, nose, and feet for doing Your will, Lord. Hallelujah!

Thank You, Father in heaven, for a quiet spirit in me. Thank You for peace that surpasses my understanding. Thank You for being the Rock of my salvation. Thank You, Father, for my husband, children, and family. Jesus, glory to Your name. Hallelujah! My Counselor, my Prince of peace, my Rose in Sharon, my Lily in the valley. Thank You, Lord. Hallelujah! No one can take Your place, Lord. You brought me through. You kept my mind.

Saints of God, the Lord is worthy to be praised. Father, I surrender this day back to You that You have given me. I worship You, Lord. Use me to Your will. Use Your entire body of Christ for Your glory, Lord! It was You, Lord, that paid the price for us to receive life eternity with You. Hallelujah!

December 22, 2019

Father, You are the Word that became flesh over two thousand years ago that we may have life eternal with You. Thank You, Jesus Christ of Nazareth. It is truly a blessing to get to know You and also get to know who I am through You. You are welcome to dwell in this earthly vessel, Lord. I belong to You. Everything I have is Yours. Lord, You are Lord over all flesh. The earth is Yours and the fullness thereof, Lord. Thank You, Emmanuel. Glory to Your holy name. I will continue to praise You both in season and out of season because You are always with me, even to the end of this world. Every knee shall bow and every tongue shall confess Jesus is Lord. It is good to know You, Lord. We are safe in Your arms. Hallelujah!

Saints of God, I am committed to getting better every day through the power of the Holy Spirit. I choose to allow God to use this earthly vessel for His glory. No man, not even me, will take credit for what the Lord is doing and has done in my life. I owe all the praise to our Lord and Savior. Will you join me on this journey to destiny? Our goal is heaven. Hallelujah! Sing, "I can only imagine." For our Lord has prepared a place to receive His bride. Thank You, Jesus. It is truly a blessing to wake up in the morning with the Lord on my mind. Yes, I am grateful to God for my husband, children, and family; however, I am most grateful for my life that I get to share with them in Christ Jesus. Even when times get tough and seems unbearable, Emmanuel is near. There is nothing that the Lord cannot do. He is Lord of hosts. Let us declare no weapon formed against us shall prosper. Amen.

December 23, 2019

Thank You, Father God, in heaven for this brand-new day that You have allowed me to experience. Lord, not only me but also all Your children are recipients of Your grace this morning. I am grateful for the blessing. My soul rejoices this morning. There is none like You, holy Father, King of kings. Lord, You are my soul provider. I celebrate You today. Hallelujah.

Saints of God, every time I turn around, the Lord is blessing us. Is this your testimony? It is my prayer that it is. Hallelujah! It's not because we have been so good, but it's because God is so good. Amen.

The Lord is a merciful Father. Who would not want to serve and worship such a powerful Almighty God. There is none like Him. I take this moment to reverence Him in His greatness. I thank You, Lord, for saving me.

Saints of God, I pray this too is your testimony, today and days to come. Glory to Your name, Lord! Hallelujah!

December 25, 2019

Thank You, Lord and Savior. Thank You, Lord Jesus. Hallelujah! Glory to Your name, Lord. I praise You. There is none like You. Father, thank You for Your love. I thank You for waking me up this morning. I thank You for my health and strength. I thank You for my husband. I thank You for our children. I thank You for our family. I thank You for the Word becoming flesh and Your Word dwelling among man to show us the way to You Father. Hallelujah!

Saints of God, let's give thanks unto our Lord. There is no failing in God. It is already done. Whatever the promise, according to the Word of God, it shall surely come to pass on earth as it is in heaven. Remember, our case has already been settled. We reject fear. Let us reject sickness and doubt. Let us reject jealousy. Let us reject sin. Let us reject wickedness. Amen.

Our time is now. Hallelujah! Glory to Your holy name, Lord. We welcome You to lead and guide us through this path of righteousness. We submit our all to You, Lord. We bless Your name. We believe in Your holy Word. We celebrate Your life, Lord. Amen.

December 27, 2019

Thank You, Lord, for this blessed day. Thank You for waking me up this morning. Thank You for my family, health, and strength. There is none like You. Thank You for Your Spirit, Lord. Some call You everlasting Father. Some call You Prince of peace, Counselor, Emmanuel. Hallelujah! You are the great I am. Thank You for saving us, Lord. We are saved by grace through faith in Jesus Christ.

My brothers and sisters in Christ, it is already done. Whatever we need, God shall supply it. Jesus paid the price that we shall live and declare the will of God for our lives on earth as it is in heaven. If we have not yet surrendered our all to Christ, this is the time to give it over to our Lord and Savior for He has already paid the price on Calvary. Amen. Come to Jesus while we still have time. Come nigh our, Lord. Amen.

January 1, 2020

Yes, Lord Almighty, great grace. Thank You, Father in heaven. There is none like You, Lord. I receive Your blessings, Lord. Hallelujah! I declare over my life and the life of my family that it's already done in Jesus name. Thank You, Jesus. I owe my all to You, Lord. Hallelujah!

Thank You, Lord, for a brand-new year. I declare that this is the year of manifestation of Your will for my life as well as desires of my heart according to Your will, Lord. Thank You, Lord, for what You have already done. Hallelujah! I declare blessing on every month of this year. I declare my husband is coming home and favor over our children as well as our entire family. For Your glory, Lord, I decree "it's already done" in Jesus name.

January 2, 2020

Thank You, Father God, in heaven for protecting my family. Thank You for waking me up this morning to find our house in peace. Thank You for keeping the robber away. I praise Your holy name, Lord. There is none like You, Lord. Hallelujah! Thank You, Father in heaven, for giving us, my family, a miracle. Thank You for protecting our body and keeping us in our right mind. I thank You, Lord, for allowing me to be victorious in my dream this morning. I thank You that no weapon formed against us shall prosper. Glory to Your holy name Jesus Christ of Nazareth, for You are Lord over my family. Our Father in heaven, hallowed be Thy name. Jehovah is Your name. Hallelujah!

Saints of God, the Lord is protecting us from all evil. He is our Good Shepherd. Even in our dreams, the Lord God Almighty is protecting us. Our Father in heaven cares. No weapon formed against us shall prosper. It's already done. It is settled. Whatever we need, God got it. Whatever we desire, God shall supply it. This is the will of God that He will get the glory, so whatever we need or desire should always be for the glory of God. Amen.

Thank You, Lord, for protecting our dreams. I thank You for reminding me, in a dream, that Your Word keeps me from being robbed. It is Your Word, Lord Almighty, that keeps the door closed to the enemy. It is Your Word that keeps Your children protected. Hallelujah!

Saints of God, everything we need is in God's Word. Remember, it's already done, but we have to pray and fast and continue to ask the Lord God Almighty (our Father in heaven) for daily bread. It is the Word of God that will sustain us in these evil days. We have to pray God's kingdom to come on earth as it is in heaven. Amen.

Thank You, Lord, for Your daily Bread. Thank You for reminding us to always remember You and know that You are our Protector. Thank You, Jesus. Thank You, Father, for being faithful even when we are lacking in our commitment to Your Word. Forgive us, Father. Have mercy on us, Lord. Saints of God, join me in staying committed to praying, fasting, and studying the Word of God. Let us not continue to rob ourselves of God's blessings. We rob ourselves when we do not heed the Word of God. We have to meditate daily. Let us not get stagnant in our walk with the Lord just because it is already done. Yes, it is already done, but we have to remain faithful until Christ comes. Amen.

January 3, 2020

Good morning, Holy Spirit. Good morning, Father, Lord God Almighty. Thank You, Lord, for all that You have already done. I magnify You on today. There is none like You, Lord. Hallelujah! Glory to God. I lean and depend on You to carry me through this day by the power of the Holy Spirit. I am an overcomer in Jesus name. My family is blessed in Jesus name. My desire shall come to pass in Jesus name. It is already done. My case has already been settled in heaven, now on earth as it is in heaven, Lord. Hallelujah! My husband is a blessed man. Our children are blessed. I am a blessed wife and mother in Jesus name. I declare we have the victory through Christ Jesus.

Saints of God, declare victory over Your lives. No matter what is going on in the world today, declare no weapon formed against the children of God shall prosper. We are in this world, but not of this world. There is safety in the arms of God Almighty. Hallelujah!

Father in heaven, protect Your children on this day. Let our hearts be protected and covered by the blood of Jesus. I plead the blood of Jesus as bloodline around the children of God. Do it for Your glory, Lord. You promised us, Father in heaven, that the righteous shall see the reward of the wicked. Vengeance is Yours, Lord. I declare that we are more than conquerors through Christ Jesus. It is already done. Amen.

January 8, 2020

Hallelujah! Glory to the Lamb of God. Thank You, Father God, in heaven for this blessed day. Thank You, Jesus, my Lord and Savior. Thank You, Holy Spirit, for abiding in me and giving me the victory. I bless Your holy name, Lord Jehovah. There is none like You, Lord. My soul rejoices in Your Word, Lord. Hallelujah! Sing, "No, never alone Lord. I'm a friend of God for He calls me friend." Hallelujah!

Saints of God, tell the devil, "Devil, you are a liar." Satan, the Lord God Almighty rebuke You, so get behind the body of Christ. I declare the Word of God over the body of Christ that no weapon formed against us shall prosper. I declare the Word of God that no evil shall befall us nor come near our dwelling as it is written. The Word of God declares us blessed. There is no failing in God. The Lord thou God is Omnipotent, all powerful. He is Yahweh. Let us continue to put our trust in Him. Hallelujah!

January 9, 2020

Thank You, Father in heaven. I believe Your Word to be true, Lord. I will continue to trust You, God Almighty. Hallelujah! Glory to Your name, Lord Jehovah. Thank You, Father, for Your Son and our Savior, Christ Jesus. Our Redeemer lives. Thank You, Lord, for allowing us to see another blessed day and protecting my family on last night. Thank You for not forgetting about Your children. Thank You, Lord, for Your Holy Spirit that reigns in our lives. I love You, Holy Spirit. Hallelujah! There is one like You Lord. It's already done.

Saints of God, let us continue to walk in expectation. Knowing that it is already done is having faith in the One that knows the ending from the beginning. We need to know that whatever God's will for our lives is, it is already done. I declare, "It's already done." Hallelujah! Join me on this path to righteousness for His name's sake. Lord, do it on earth as it is in heaven. Father God, help us with our heart's desires that it lines up with Your desire that You will for us. I reject doubt and unbelief. I walk in liberty and truth. My faith has made me whole. Come on, saints, declare the word over your lives as well. This life that I now live, I live in Christ Jesus. There is none like You, Lord. Hallelujah!

January 16, 2020

Hallelujah! Praise ya! I feel Your presence, Lord. Thank You, Father in heaven. Thank You for Your indwelling power. I trust You, Lord. You are faithful. There is none like You. Glory to Your holy name. Jehovah is Your name. Amen.

Saints of God, stay encouraged. The Lord will never leave nor forsake us. Hold on to the Word of God. Our Father in heaven is a faithful God. There is none like You, Lord. Say it with me, "There is none like Jehovah." Jesus is Lord over our life. We have an advocate in heaven. His name is Emmanuel. We are never alone. There is power in the name of Jesus.

This is actually the fourth day of my forty-day fast. I was not going to share it, but I was led to share this personal and powerful moment with you. We are family. There is nothing wrong with practicing what we preach. I am determined to see the power of God move in our lives as never before. So, at this point, why not join me on fasting, praying, and giving of our service for the glory of God to move in our lives to advance the kingdom of God? It is only my fourth day, and I am already seeing the power of God moving in my family. My family has heard good news from the NVC, our lawyer, our accountant, and our children already. It is the Lord's doing. He is marvelous. Even our paralegal reports that our case has been progressing smoothly. She encouraged us to continue to be patient. We will not fail. Hallelujah!

January 18, 2020

Good morning, Holy Spirit. Father in heaven, I worship You. Lord Jesus Christ, my Lord and Savior, I thank You. Thank You, God Almighty, for saving me from a burning pit of hell. Thank You for saving my family and every child of God. Hallelujah! You are worthy, Lord. I put my trust in You, Lord. You are a miracle worker,

Lord. Your name is Yahweh. Hallelujah! I praise You, Lord. Thank You. Thank You. Thank You, Lord. Bring glory to Your name, Lord. Hallelujah!

> But Israel shall be saved in the Lord with an everlasting Salvation; ye shall not be ashamed nor confounded world without end. For thus saith the Lord that created the heavens; God himself that formed the earth and made it, he hath established it, he created it not in vain, he formed it to be inhabited; I am the Lord; and there is none else. (Isaiah 45:17–18)

> Look unto me, and be ye saved, all the ends of the earth: For I am God, and there is none else. (Isaiah 45:22)

> For I am not ashamed of the gospel of Christ: for it is the Power of God unto salvation to everyone that believeth to the Jew first; and, also, to the Greek. (Romans 1:16)

Father God, in heaven, thank You for your spoken Word today. Thank You, Lord, for reminding me to only stay focus on what You Word says concerning my life and the lives of all Your children.

Saints of God, I am encouraged by the Word of God. Let me encourage You today. God Almighty is good. The Lord is faithful concerning our lives, if we will only listen and obey His Word. I love the way that our Lord encourages our hearts, if we will turn to Him and key our mind on His Word. The Word is the Will of God on earth as it is in heaven. We have to stay focused and trust God's Word. The Word is in our hearts as children of God. I thank the heavenly Father for abiding in me. Isn't it amazing how Jesus Christ, our Lord, already paid the price in full that we only have to believe and confess the Him as our Lord and Savior. This is why He is King of kings, Lord of lords, and Lord of hosts. Hallelujah! This is why

He's now sitting with the Father interceding for us, having prepared a place, so that He may receive us to His glory. Jesus is coming soon, saints, to receive us, and He's coming with His reward with Him. He paid the ransom. Hallelujah!

My brothers and sisters who are in Christ Jesus, this is why my heart is merry no matter what challenges we may be facing. It's nothing compared to the glory that will be revealed through Christ. Confess His Word over our life without ceasing. I am not ashamed of the gospel. Say it with me, "We are not ashamed of the gospel of Jesus Christ!" Hallelujah!

If you all can recall, just a couple of days ago, I was given thanks for good news that was shared on my family's behalf from the NVC. My husband and I had gotten a couple of e-mails from the NVC that announced all our documents received and was now qualified for the US consular in Accra, Ghana. It was confirmed by our lawyer's office as well, but yesterday, I received another e-mail from the lawyer's office that indicated that my income did not meet the criteria to sponsor my husband.

I actually was at work when I received this update. My day was a bit overwhelming. I had not had lunch, and we were already over into the afternoon. I was nearing exhaustion by this time. I looked at my e-mail, and this was what I saw. Why am I sharing this? Because any other time, I would have panicked and started to worry with this kind of news. It was totally opposite of the good news that we received just two days ago that I was eager to share with you all. What would be your response at this point? Exactly! Say it with me, "But God!" Hallelujah! Glory to the Lamb of God. Thank You, Jesus. My response is and will be to praise our Father in heaven. Sing, "I come too far to turn around." Hallelujah!

His name is Yahweh, a miracle worker. I woke up singing this song this morning. My soul rejoiced in the Lord. When faced with adversity, we can look to our Father in heaven. Remember, I also shared with you a couple of days ago that I was fasting. It was my fourth day remember. Yes, exactly. The Lord Almighty had already foreseen my challenges and had gone on before me to make my path straight. Hallelujah! This is why I am sharing this testimony with you all. Some things come only through fasting and praying. Hallelujah! I can stop right there, but there is more to the story. We all shall witness the manifestation of God's miracle. What seems impossible to man is made possible with the help of Almighty God. There is nothing too hard for our Lord. When faced with sudden adversity, we can remember "now faith" as it is written in Hebrews 11:1. The Lord already knows what we stand in need of before we need.

Whose report will we believe? I know what man says concerning our case, but more than this, I know what our Father in heaven showed me already and spoken to me concerning our case. The Word of the Lord to me is still "it's already done." My time is now. Our time is now! The Word has already gone before us. Do you believe? I believe God's report. I believe the Word of God. No weapon formed against my family shall prosper. It is the Lord's will that man leaves his mother and father and cleaves to his wife. That's the will of God. Nothing shall separate us from the Lord of God. That's the will of God. Hallelujah!

My husband always tells me, "God gives good gifts to His children." Now if the report is not according to the Word of God, I do not receive it. "Now faith" is my motto no matter what the circumstances are. I will trust God at His Word. I will lift up the name of Jesus. I will, by the power of the Holy Spirit, remember God's Word concerning my life. It is my prayer that you will join me on this road of "now faith." There is no room for fear or this road, only the reverence our Lord and Savior beholding His glory. Remember, we are saved by grace through faith in our Lord and Savior Jesus Christ. Salvation is of the Lord and available to all that believe and confess. Amen.

> For every one that asketh receiveth; and he that seeketh findeth; and to him that knocketh it shall be open. Or what man is there of you, whom if his son ask bread, will he give him a stone? Or if he ask a fish, will he give him, a serpent? If ye then, being evil, know how to give good gifts to your children, how much more shall

your Father which is in Heaven give good things
to them that ask him? (Matthew 7:8–11)

Such a powerful word! Hallelujah! This Word confirms what
my husband always instills in me. God gave good gifts to His people.
Thank You, Holy Spirit, for bringing the Word of God back to my
memory in times like these. It's already done! God's Word is available
to all that receive. I can hear the Lord say, "Come unto Me!"

It is my prayer that every reader is being blessed by these testimonies, thanksgivings, and the Word of God as we journey together
to experience the miracle of God. It's all for His glory. Do it, Lord,
for your name's sake. I pray blessings over every reader. God bless and
keep us all. This is the will of God. Amen.

January 21, 2020

Hallelujah! Glory to Your name, Lord. Father in heaven, You
are worthy of all the praise. Thank You for waking me up this morning. There is none like You, Lord. I thank You for my family. I thank
You for my health and strength. I thank You for my mind. I thank
You for my husband and our children. I thank You for grace and
mercy, Lord. Glory!

Saints of God, to be totally honest to myself and you all, the last
few days have been both a challenge and victorious. The Lord keeps
seeing me through. It's my prayer that He is doing the same in Your
lives as well. I am determined to finish this journey with victory in
Jesus, my Savior forever. I can hear my late mom singing that melody
in my ears even as I write this morning. I believe the Lord Almighty
is going to see us through. I pray that this is your desire as well. What
are you believing God for? What man may see as impossible, but
God Almighty is the God of the impossible. He's a miracle worker.
He specializes in things that are impossible. I will never give up on
God. I pray that this is your testimony as well. Hallelujah! God is
love. The Lord loves his children so much. Satan is the father of
lies. Whose report are we going to believe? Let's show our Father in
heaven our gratitude for the love that He has not only shown us but

also given us through the life of His only begotten Son, Jesus Christ. Hallelujah!

Yesterday, I received a phone call from our lawyer's office. No, it was not what we were expecting. The paralegal, from the office, proceeded to tell me that we (me and my husband) had not done anything wrong, but she said the NVC was saying that my income did not meet the requirement to sponsor my husband to come home to me. This was the message that we had been getting over these last few days, but only to find out that (according to the national requirements) my income was more than triple the minimum requirements. So what was the problem? The devil is a liar. The lawyer's office recommended that we go back and amend our taxes and file without my husband in 2018 although that's the year of our marriage. They also recommended that I get a cosponsor to assist or complement my income. I am in no way confused about these recommendations.

At this point, I am looking right past this conversation and telling the devil he is a liar. From day one, both me and my husband have been honest to the best of our ability and heeded all the recommendations and met the requirements that had been asked of us. This process has been very lengthy, but the Lord Almighty has been standing in the gap for us and making a way even when there seems to be no way. When we first started, we were told that this journey, at the most, would take about six to nine months, but in May of this year, it would be two years since we initially filed with USCIS office. It's only by the grace of God that we are growing stronger in our marriage and faith in God's Word. We are trusting in God with all our hearts. We believe God's report. Hallelujah! We love the Lord so much. That same love we share by the grace of God. Hallelujah!

It was just this past September that I was led by the Spirit of God to just simply start writing this journey. This journey, as we all can recall, started with a similar miracle. As we recall, man's report then was that we needed more evidence; however, God's report was, "Your case has been approved," without more evidence. Hallelujah! Now, here we are again with man's report that we need more evidence of support. Our Father in heaven has not changed His mind. He is the same yesterday, today, and forevermore. Glory to God! His Word has not return back unto Him void, nor has He forgotten His promise for our lives. Whose report will we believe? Yes, the devil is trying to distract us again, but I am encouraged. I can also hear my husband's voice, "Our Father gives good gifts to His children." Amen.

Saints of God, our answer to our lawyer's office was as follows: we have done all we know how to do in this case. We have done everything that was asked of us up until this date. We have patiently waited throughout this process. We are sorry to hear that it's now being recommended that we amend our taxes and get a cosponsor when we were indeed married in 2018, and my income exceeded the minimum requirements to sponsor him. Our answer was, "No no no!" No, thank you! God bless our lawyer and all the staff. We know they probably meant well, but no! This is our lives that we are talking about.

We knew that there was no way other than God's way to do this. We just didn't understand what the problem was. The paralegal even went as far to make the comment that it's probably due to the country that my husband was immigrating from. Wow! I was not going to even address this further due to the nature of this journey and our need to stay focused on our promise. Hallelujah! The last thing that I said to the paralegal concerning this matter was, "God is in control." We just had to wait and see, and while waiting, I asked the Lord to prove them doubters wrong. We bless them. It is times like this that we need to remember who we are in Christ Jesus. We need to know our inheritance. Jehovah is His name! Hallelujah!

January 24, 2020

For Your glory, Father in heaven, I lift up the name of Jesus Christ of Nazareth. Father, draw all men unto Thee. I thank You, God Almighty. I love You, Father. There is none like You in heaven or earth. Hallelujah! I bless Your holy name. My soul rejoices in Your Word. Glory to God!

Saints of God, help me lift our Savior up. We all belong to God Almighty. His very breath fills us. Thank You, Holy Spirit. Hallelujah! This is the day that the Lord has made. We will rejoice and be glad in it. Amen. We have an advocate that is near unto us, and His name is Jesus. There is power in His name. We have a comforter that is near unto us, and His name is the Holy Spirit. We have a heavenly Father, and His name is Jehovah. Some call Him Yahweh, some Elohim, some El Shaddai, some I AM, some El Roi, and so on. Hallelujah! HE is LORD. Hallelujah! When we call on JESUS CHRIST, the Lord hears us. Amen. Help me lift HIM up, saints. Hallelujah!

January 27, 2020

Glory to God. Praise yah! Praise yah! Hallelujah! Thank You, heavenly Father, for my Lord and Savior, Jesus Christ. Thank You, Father, for the Holy Spirit. There is no one else like You, Lord. Thank You for laying the foundation of your Word in the lives of your children. Hallelujah!

Saints of God, I am encouraged today by the Word of God. The Lord promised to never leave nor forsake us. The presence and mere essence of our Lord is here. I receive the blessing this morning. It is my prayer that you too will receive God's blessing today. Help me say it, "It's already done." Hallelujah! I remember just like yesterday. Thank You, Holy Spirit, for reminding me today when you first spoke those words to me. I feel Your presence this morning, Holy Spirit, for You are truly my Helper. Hallelujah! God, You are so clever. Your timing, Father, is the best timing. Your answer is yes and amen. No one can encourage me like You can, Father, but I truly thank You for using the lives of Your children to bless Your children. Knowing that this is truly a God's thing, no one can compare to You, Lord. Your favor is perfect. Your timing is perfect. All we, as your children, have to do is believe and obey Your Word. Hallelujah!

Saints of God, I am encouraged. Please do not take it lightly when the Lord places you on another believer's mind and that person decides to reach out to check on you. Please do not take it lightly when that person is you that the Lord is leading to reach out to check on another believer in Christ. We never know what that person is dealing with at that particular time. We have to be sensitive to the Holy Spirit. Amen. I said that to say, this morning, I woke up with the desire to be encourage today. I got up searching for one of my best books on the promises of God for our every need. There it was located on my desk. It's one of the smallest books in my collection but carries the most powerful promises of God that will change any negative thoughts to positive and productive thoughts that will also ignite to fire of God in our lives. Our Father wants us to want what He wants and say what He says and do what He does concerning our lives. Hallelujah!

Today, I received a text message from a former pastor. The text message just simply said, "Praise God. I'm just checking on you." That's all it said, but it was so powerful and encouraging this morning because I knew that it was by the Spirit of God. It felt like a father's message to his daughter. It was very few in words, but those words were much needed this morning. Thank You, heavenly Father, for speaking through one of your sons today to answer the desire of one of your daughters. Lord, You not only encouraged me today but also reminded me of where it all began in You, Lord. It was under this former ministry when the Lord first spoke the Word of promise directly to me from heaven. That Word was and still is "it's already done." Hallelujah! Praise God!

I remember just joining that ministry. I got up to walk from the altar back to my chair and heard, "It's already done," along with what sounds like an army of angels marching in my ears. That had to be at least ten to twelve years ago. I did not realize it, at that time, those words actually came right before some major attacks from the enemy in my life that would leave me feeling deserted and defeated; however, the Lord had a greater plan for my life. I can see much clearer today and still am reminded of those words, "It's already done." Hallelujah! It is only by grace that I am still here to tell of the Lord's goodness and mercy. Hallelujah!

> For all the promises of God in him are yea,
> and in him Amen, unto the glory of God by us.
> (2 Corinthians 1:20)

Whereby, when ye read, ye may understand
my knowledge in the mystery of Christ) Which
in other ages was not made known unto the sons
of men, as it is now revealed unto his holy apos-
tles and prophets by the Spirit; That the Gentiles
should be fellowheirs, and of the same body, and
partakers of his promise in Christ by the gospel.
(Ephesians 3:4–6)

Saints of God, sometimes we might not physically see the plan of God working in our lives, but that does not mean that His plan is not being fulfilled. Join me on this happy road to destiny as we journey through this life with Christ. Remember, we are not walking alone. The power of God is with us. We are fellowheirs with Christ. The Holy Spirit is our comforter and guide. Have we read? We know the ending from the beginning, remember? Hallelujah! "It's already done!" Glory to God. There is no failing in God. Let us walk together with Christ Jesus for He knows the way. Jesus Christ is the way to our heavenly Father. This is our ultimate goal. Let us continue to declare the Word of God over our lives and the lives of every believer of God. Let's remind Jehovah, "Your Word is a lamp to my feet and a light to my path" (Psalm 119:105). Hallelujah! It's already done in Jesus name.

February 5, 2020

Good morning, Holy Spirit. It is my prayer that You lead and guide me today. I pray for the manifestation of Your power, Lord. Thank You, Father in heaven, for Your miracle today. Thank You, Jesus, my Lord and Savior. There is none like You, Lord. Hallelujah! Praise Your holy name. Father in heaven, I thank You for what You are doing in this season. Thank You for drawing Your people back to You, Lord. Father God, You are amazing. There is none like You. Lord, I ask You to locate Your children today and strengthen us with Your anointing. It is Your anointing that destroy the yoke.

Saints of God, hold on to the Word of God. Let us continue to walk together and believe God for His promises. Let us continue to fast, pray, and obey the Word of God so that we will be blessed and He can use us for His will on earth as it is in heaven. Devil, you no longer reign in the lives of the children of God. Satan, your days are coming to an end in Jesus name. I declare victory over the children of God Almighty. My dear brothers and sisters in Christ, let us exercise the gifts that God has given us, and among them, let's put on the whole armor of God so we can stand against the wrath of our enemy in Jesus name as it is written. Hallelujah!

February 7, 2020

Hallelujah! Glory to Your name, Lord Jehovah. We bless Your name, Lord. Thank You, Jesus Christ, our Savior. Our souls rejoice in You, Lord. We are not alone. Thank You, Holy Spirit, for Your comfort and guide this morning. This is the day that You, Lord, have made. We will rejoice and be glad in it. Hallelujah!

Saints of God, this is our opportunity to give God some praise. Hallelujah! I feel the power of God moving on the inside of me. My prayer that this too is your testimony. Come on and let us praise God this morning. Glory to Your name, Lord. Victory belongs to Jesus. There is victory in Jesus, our Savior, forever. Glory to God! Thank You, Lord. It is already done. Say it with me, "It is done in Jesus name!" Amen. We are truly living just to live again. I am grasping the meaning of this concept as my days are lengthened and strengthened by the Word of God. My husband always tells me, "God gives good gifts to His children." Now, I find myself ministering to others the same Word of encouragement. Our God is faithful. Let us continue to believe God at His Word. Say it with me, "God gives good gifts to His children." Hallelujah! Now, let us meditate on this Word and receive it together. Amen.

It's already done. Say it again with me, "It's already done." Do you believe it? I believe God. Let us believe God together. Our Father in heaven is intentional. Let us not be distracted by man's report if it doesn't line up with the Word of God. What is our Lord saying in our situation? Do we have our case before the Lord Jehovah? He is the same God yesterday, today, and forevermore. Hallelujah! We can do whatever we put our minds and hearts to because our Father created us in His image and likeness, but all we do or desire should be for the glory of God. What does the Word of God say about our lives? We want from God, but do we deserve what He has for us? Are we totally committed to the will of our Father in heaven? Do we have church in us? Do we acknowledge our Father in heaven? Is our Lord pleased with us?

Every so often, there is nothing wrong with assessing our "now." Where are we now? Are we growing in Christ? Do we believe in the entire Word of God? The Bible clearly tells us that some will have the form of godliness but will deny the power thereof. The Word doesn't lie. The Word is Truth. Hallelujah! Glory to God. I remember when that used to be my story, but "now" my testimony is "new." I am new in Christ. All things become "new" in Christ Jesus. Hallelujah!

Saints of God, what is it going to take for us all to believe and receive the gifts of our Father in heaven? If the Word of God tells us that "it's already done," why do we not trust God at all times? I urge you to join me on this journey with Christ Jesus and live a life of victory in every aspect of our lives the way that God Almighty intended from the beginning. Remember, "it's already done" from the beginning. If it is love that we need, God first loved the world that He gave us our Lord and Savior Jesus Christ unto salvation. Hallelujah!

The Bible tells us the same was in the beginning, and God said, "Let's create man in our image." Who is "our"? We, as children of God, know that "our" is the Father, Son, and the Holy Spirit. Amen. Hallelujah!

In the beginning, we were created by God Almighty. He placed everything we need on the inside of us in the beginning. Through Christ Jesus, all that seem lost has been restored same as the beginning. Hallelujah! So why, as believers, do we struggle with just simply believing God and walking with the Holy Spirit until our Savior Jesus returns. He shall surely come quickly. Knowing who we are in Christ and who we belong to is God's will for our lives. Let us pull on heaven in prayer, fasting, and obedience. Let us walk together in unity. Amen.

February 10, 2020

Hallelujah! Glory to Your name, Lord! There is none like You, Lord. Praise Your name. Thank You, Father in heaven. Thank You, Lord Jesus. Thank You, Holy Spirit. I believe Your Word, Lord. Do it for Your glory, Lord!

Saints of God, all has not been told, but today I am going to continue to take the high road with Christ Jesus. Victory has my name on it in Christ Jesus's name. This journey has become so personal for me. I am going to either continue to trust God's plan for my life or forfeit what He has already done. What about you? What are you believing God for that has yet to manifest? I mean, we can imagine it and believe it, but what about seeing the evidence of our faith. Well, just like myself, I urge you to hold on because help is on the way. Satan has no grip on our destiny. Our Father has mapped out a great plan for our lives, and it shall surely come to pass in Jesus name. Hallelujah!

So let us not even waste our time nor energy on anything other than what we are believing God for. Say it with me, "It shall surely come to pass in Jesus name." Hallelujah! Glory to Your name, Lord. Two is better than one. One of us is bound to testify any day now. Glory to God! Let us continue to celebrate what God has already done. It is my prayer that you are feeling better right now concerning your desire or request that you have before God Almighty. I am feeling pretty good as we speak. It's raining outside. This rain is a good sign of life more abundantly. It is a sign of overflow. It's a sign of constant flow in our lives, just like our blessing from God Almighty. It's raining in our lives. Just because we do not see the rain somedays does not mean that the rain is shut up. It's just waiting for the right atmosphere to fall down. All we have to do is believe and the rain will fall at the right time.

MY DECLARATIONS

I declare that our days of drought are over.
I declare that our days are full of blessings.
I declare that we have victory through Christ Jesus.
I declare that our marriages are blessed.
I declare that our health is blessed.
I declare that our finances are blessed.
I declare that no weapon formed against us shall prosper.
I declare that our enemies will scatter and be defeated.
I declare victory over our circumstances.
I declare that we are blessed going and coming.
Hallelujah!

Help me, saints, to declare the promises of God over our lives. I declare that we will not get weary in doing. This is our season. It's already done. Father in heaven, prove the doubters wrong. You are God and God all by yourself. Your name is Jehovah. Hallelujah!

IT IS TIME

Glory to God. Good morning, Holy Spirit. Thank You, Lord Jehovah. Thank You, Jesus Christ of Nazareth. Thank You, Father God. Hallelujah! I receive Your Word, Lord. Glory glory glory! Thank You, Lord, for the miracle. There is none like You, Lord. I believe Your Word, Lord. Hallelujah! For Your glory, Lord. There is no limit in what You can do, Lord. Your name is Yahweh. Sweet Holy Spirit of God, have Your way. I give You glory, Lord. Glory to Your name, Lord. Jesus is Lord. Hallelujah!

Saints of God, now is the time to receive the blessing of God. "It's time," said the spirit of the Lord to me this morning while meditating on His Word. It's my prayer that you too receive this word from the Lord. It is time. Hallelujah! We have waited patiently on God. I do not know what you have been believing God Almighty for, but His name is wonderful. He is a mighty Counselor. The Lord gives good gifts to His children. Actually, I truly thought that the final chapter of this book was "It's Already Done," but while meditating on the Word of God this morning, the Holy Spirit has given me another chapter to start writing on as you see, "It Is Time." Hallelujah! Glory to God. I know in my soul that "it's time." Say it with me, "It's time." Hallelujah!

It goes to show us that God is not through with us yet. We serve a mighty God, our heavenly Father. There is none like Him. I truly thank the Lord for the miracle that He has performed in my life, and I pray that this is your testimony as well. This truly has been an awesome experience as we walk with the Spirit of God. Just to know and be reassured that we are not alone is encouraging. The Lord will never leave nor forsake us. We have to be with God. Trust God, saints. Let us continue to trust His plan for our lives even if we do not physically see it. Trust God and let's continue to ask Him to let His will for our lives be done on earth as it is in heaven. Hallelujah!

It takes a strong person to endure the cares of this world, but through the power of the Holy Spirit, we will continue to be victorious. Do you believe? I believe. If the Lord says, "It's time," then it's time. Now, do I know all the details? No. Do you know all the details? No. Does our Lord Almighty know all the details? Yes! Hallelujah! Glory to God. All we have to do is trust our Father and believe His Word that has been spoken to us. It is time. It is time. It is time. In the name of Jesus, it is time. No shaking. No bending. No doubt. It is time. It is written, "Arise and shine; for thy light is come, and the glory of the Lord is risen upon thee" (Isaiah 60:1). Amen.

February 18, 2020

Thank You, Father God, in heaven. Lord, I love You. I acknowledge Your presence. There is none like You, Lord. Hallelujah! Bless Your name, Lord. I need Thee, oh Lord. I praise Your Holy name. Thank You, Jesus. You have made a way, Lord. Glory to Your name. Lord, You are good and Your mercy endureth forever. Hallelujah!

Saints of God, let us join together and thank God for "now faith." Let us thank Him for what He has already done. It is time for us to resist the devil and no longer let him have dominion over our minds, our bodies, our families, and our desires. God gives good gifts to his children. That's the Word. Let us believe God's Word. No shaking. No breaking. No bending. Let us edify one another and pray for one another lest we fall. God inhabits the praises of His people as it is written. I called on the Lord, and He heard my cry. Hallelujah. I have decided to trust the Word of God no matter how I feel or what I see. I pray that this too is your story. "Now faith" is my testimony.

Hallelujah! Glory to God. I praise You, Lord. Thank You. Thank You. Thank You, Lord. Lord, You are faithful. My soul rejoices in the Word. Thank You, Jesus. Yes to Your will, Lord. Thank You for Your answered prayers. Victory in Jesus, my Savior forever. Hallelujah.

Saints of God, my soul rejoices this morning. Trust God with all your hearts. God is faithful. His Word will not return back unto Him void. Hallelujah! I cannot explain, with words, how I feel this morning. I can only try to explain, but believe me when I tell you that all has not been told. Glory to God. This has been an amazing journey that I have embarked upon by the grace of God. Father, I thank You for Your Spirit. I thank You, Lord, for being holy and for Your desire for us to be a holy people. I thank You for desiring to best for Your children, Lord. Hallelujah! It is truly my prayer that you all can feel the Spirit of God, and I hope you are encouraged to give God some praise for what He has already done.

Reality check. Just because the Lord has given us a word does not mean that everyone you share the Word with will receive it or will be excited about it as you are. Hallelujah!

Saints of God, as believers of God's Word, we have to be good stewards of the Word. We all have a right to the Word of God. There is no respect of person. Remember, the Word of God is still going forth. We have to grab hold to the Word of God. The Lord is speaking every day through the Word of God. The time is "now." The Bible tells us that the Lord is our Shepherd, and the Lord's sheep knows His voice as it is written. The more we commune with God, the more we know His voice. What is the Lord saying in this hour? What time of the season are we in? What have we been believing God for? Are we good watchman of the Word of God?

For example, look at the life of Noah. Not many believed in the word that the Lord had given him, but Noah believed. Noah persevered because he trusted God. The time finally came when God's Word manifested. It was as if day and night came at the same hour. Noah received the revelation, and his family was saved from the flood. What appeared as day for them was night for others who did not believe. Have mercy, Lord!

For example, look at the response of the disciples the hour before Jesus, our Lord, was taken by the soldiers from the chief priests and pharisees. While Jesus prayed, the disciples slept.

> And he came out, and went, as he was wont, to the mount of Olives; and his disciples also followed him. And when he was at the place, he said unto them, Pray that ye enter not into temptation. And when he rose up from prayer, and was come to his disciples, he found them sleeping for sorrow, And said unto them, why sleep ye? Rise and pray, lest ye enter into temptation. (Luke 22:39–40, 45–46)

The Word of the Lord has been tailored fit for all of God's children. Hallelujah! It's all for the glory of God to be revealed to us. Hallelujah! Remember, our Father does not want us walking in the darkness. Jesus is the Light. Jesus is the Way. Jesus is our Shepherd, and we shall not want. Hallelujah! I am looking for God's blessings. I am going to get my blessings. I am awake. It's time to believe God for our "now faith." The beauty of this journey is just simply trusting God. I truly thank God for how far He has brought me. Learning to trust God has been the most amazing experience. True deliverance comes when we choose to trust God no matter what comes our way. It is truly an amazing experience. It is one that pays off spiritually, emotionally, and physically. It's all about allowing the Lord to shine bright as the sun in us, allowing the Son's glory to be revealed through our lives. There is no greater love. I received this word as a word of confirmation. You see, I still believed God. I did not limit His Word to just a physical blessing. The Lord is our everlasting Father. Hallelujah! His Word supersedes what we can see and touch. Remember, He is limitless. Hallelujah! His Word is eternal. I truly pray that you all understand what I am saying as well as not saying at the same time through the Spirit of God. Hallelujah! Glory to God. Praise Your name, Lord. I give you glory, God. Your name is Yahweh.

"Marcia, what are you saying here?" I am saying that we cannot limit our Father in heaven to just giving us the desires of our hearts. We have to believe the Word of God for exactly what it says.

> But as it is written, Eye hath not seen, nor ear heard, neither have entered into the heart of man, the things which God hath prepared for them that Love him. But God hath revealed them unto us be His Spirit: for the Spirit searches all things, yea, the deep things of God. (1 Corinthians 2:9–10)

You see, saints, we serve an everlasting Father that knows all. Only by the power of the Holy Spirit can God reveal the things that He has prepared for us. It is the Spirit of God that searches our hearts. Hallelujah! Glory to God. Our Father knows best. He will never leave nor forsake us. The Lord is getting us ready for that great day. Everything the Lord is doing in our lives and through our lives is leading us closer toward Him. Jesus, our Lord and Savior, is soon to come back again. Only God knows. Let us stay awake, stay watchful, stay in the Spirit of God, and walk in our inheritance as children of God. God has said yes. Hallelujah! Who can say no? No one. Our everlasting Father is faithful to His Word. It is final. Amen.

Hearing God's voice supersedes anything that we receive physically. Being able to hear the voice of the Lord makes the things that we receive physically small compared to the things that he has prepared for us. Even though our desires look small, we cannot despise small beginnings. The Lord has prepared the way for us. It is the Lord's doing. Even though I couldn't see it before, I still believe God, just as Noah believed the Lord and the Lord spared His family from the flood. Also, Jesus warned the disciples not to fall asleep lest they be tempted or fall into temptation. We today have to take note from what has been written. We have to stay present through the Spirit of God and trust God. The Word of God is final. The Word will not return back unto Him void. Hear what the Spirit of God is saying to us and stay awake, pray, and believe. Hallelujah!

February 25, 2020

Good morning, Holy Spirit. Father God, in heaven, I worship You for You are worthy of the praise. Hallelujah! Praise Your holy name, Jehovah. Glory to God! Thank You, Jesus, for all You have done. Bless Your name, Lord. There is none like You, Lord. Lord, I stretch my hands toward heaven. I need Thee, oh Lord. I ask for divine wisdom today, Lord. I ask that You will show me the way, Lord. Guide me, Jehovah. Let Your rod and staff comfort me. Show up in my life mightily on today. Father in heaven, it is Your Word that will keep me and continue to bless me on my daily journey. Lord, keep my heart pure. I ask You, Lord, to forgive me of all my trespasses and give me the heart to forgive those who have trespass against me. Thank You, Lord. Create in me a clean heart, my Lord, and renew the right spirit in me. Hallelujah! I receive Your healing today. I receive Your deliverance today. I receive Your miracle today. I receive it all in the mighty name of Jesus Christ of Nazareth. Amen.

Father, You are my Bread of life. My life is sustained because of You. I owe You my life as a living sacrifice. I freely give You my life, Lord. I freely receive the life that you, my Lord, have given me through Christ, my Savior. Thank You, Father in heaven.

Saints of God, we have the right to praise God. There is so much that the Lord God Almighty is doing in our favor that we do not know. The Lord has our backs. All we have to do is trust God. Let this concept be our final answer unto our Lord. Say it with me, "Lord, I trust you." Hallelujah! Who is on the Lord's side? Let it be you and me. Let us stay steadfast in believing the Word of God. We are a part of God's body. We are a team. That is final. The Lord Almighty is on our side. We have a Righteous Judge as our advocate. He is King of kings. He is Lord of lords. He is Lod of host. Who does not want to be on the Lord's side? We are on the winning team. Hallelujah! Glory to Your name, Lord!

Saints of God, by now, we all should be encouraged to just simply keep on keeping on. What can the enemy do to us if we have made the Lord Jesus our choice? There is absolutely no failing in God. The Bible tells us that we are like sheep in the slaughter. The Bible tells us that we are like a flower that fades away. What is that saying to us? It means that it is a season for these earthly vessels, so what really matters is what we do for Christ Jesus, our Lord, who has paid the price that we not only live victorious but also live a life of eternity through Him. The Word of God is final. The Word of God is true. The Word of God is pure. The Word of God became flesh and dwelt among us. The Word of God is our answer. Amen.

Saints of God, the devil is a liar, and Satan is the father of lies. Who wants to serve a liar or worship the father of lies? Who wants to be led down the path to destruction? Who wants to burn in the lake of fire? Who, saints? I do not want this for myself, family, nor the entire body of Christ. Let us repent of sins seen and unseen. Our God has the "FINAL SAY." The answer is in the WORD of GOD. HALLELUJAH! This is all the reason that we should spend more time praising and worshiping our Lord and Savior rather than worrying and complaining about what's happening in between our victory. "Haven't we read the scriptures?" said the spirit of the Lord. Have we not read?

Saints of God, truth be told, we know the differences between the truth and a lie. We know the difference between good and evil. We know the difference between light and darkness. We know the difference between life and death. We must activate our faith and stand on the Word of God. The Word of God is final.

Saints of God, let us spend these last days getting to know our Father in heaven better. Our heart's desire is final only if we delight ourselves in the Lord. Do we see how much God loves us? He loves us so much. He loves us so much that He trusts us with our heart's desire when we delight ourself in His Word. Jesus Christ is the Way. We are His sheep. His sheep knows His voice. Hallelujah!

TESTIMONY

In contrast to the Word that I received, yesterday also was the first day the Supreme Court implemented the public charge (also known as the final rule) to the low-income immigrants or inspiring immigrants of United States. Thank God Almighty for opening my eyes with Your spoken Word. I am overjoyed this morning by the power of the Holy Spirit. The devil is a liar. God Almighty has already spoken from the beginning.

Saints of God, this is why it was necessary for the Lord to reveal His promised word over my heart's desire. It all makes sense now. This is why there was an urgency in my heart to fast and pray after the initial Word of God came to me. I was led to fast, pray, praise, and worship the same night, not that my Lord was withholding no good thing from me, but that He wanted me to stand on His Word no matter what I saw with my physical eyes or heard with my physical ears. Saints of God, we must be taught, by the Holy Spirit, on how to see and hear beyond what we physically see and hear. Most of all, we have to trust the Lord with all our hearts as it is written. Amen. Let us wear this "new man in Christ" well. Amen. Hallelujah! We are a team. Lord, do it. Hallelujah!

Come on church, we are in this world, but not of this world. God's ways and thoughts are greater than ours. We have to know our inheritance from the beginning and meditate on the Word of God both day and night. Even as I share with you all, I am being delivered and set free as well from the residue of bondage. We have to let our minds be also in Christ. Hallelujah! Just because we might not see our desire today does not mean that it is not done. Our case has already been settled in our favor in heaven. We have to rejoice and be exceedingly glad for what the Lord has already done from the beginning. Amen.

Saints of God, let us not believe the hype, as the younger generation would say. Let us only believe the Word of God. Jehovah is our Righteous Judge. When He says yes, who can say no? We have been charged by our Lord to keep the faith. Faith comes by the Word of God. Our Father in heaven has all power of heaven and earth.

Hallelujah! Our Father has given His only begotten Son Jesus, our Lord, power over all flesh. Our Lord and Savior, Jesus Christ, has given us power of the Word of God to apply to our lives that we become victorious through Him. Hallelujah!

Saints of God, no matter what the Supreme Court's ruling yesterday, it can be overturned at the will of God. Man's ruling is not final, but God's word is final from the beginning. In other words, God's Word will always supersede man's ruling. It has been spoken from the beginning. It is already done. The Lord is in control. Elohim has spoken from the beginning. The Word will not fail. The Word is final. Let us stand on God's Word. The Word is working for the good of those who love the Lord. Hallelujah! God bless us all. Amen.

A NEW DAY DAWNING

Thank You, Father God Almighty for this day that You have made. I will rejoice and be glad in it. Thank You, Father God, for the release of this day, "a new day dawning." Hallelujah! For we have won again. Glory to God. Hallelujah! For we have won again. Glory to God. Hallelujah! Waymaker. Promise Keeper. Glory to God. All for Your glory, Lord.

Saints of God, all has not been told. This is the day that the Lord has given us. Let us rejoice and be glad in it. I feel the power of the living God this morning. The Lord has confirmed it over and over again by the mouths of two or three witnesses that "it is time." The Lord has revealed this word to us. Hallelujah! Hallelujah! Hallelujah! Hear the Word of the Lord and receive His Word. This is "a new day dawning." Glory to God! I am excited about your future, those that can hear the Word of the Lord and believe God's Word. Yes to your will, Lord. Hallelujah! Say it with me, "Yes, Lord!" No looking back. Walking in expectation. No more delay. It's already done in Jesus name. You have to stay the course. You have walked through the wilderness. It is here, saints. Amen.

Just today, while in prayer, the Lord has given me His word to release into someone's life that is totally a senior to me on the gospel. All has not been told, but what I would like for you (the readers) to remember is that our God is faithful to His children and obedience is better than sacrifice. We are so loved by our Father. Jesus is Lord over our lives. The Holy Spirit is our guide. Most people get distracted after experiencing even a smaller part of what I have experience just today alone, but I will not be distracted because all the glory belong to God and He wants to do more. Amen.

Hallelujah! Glory to God. Lord, You are worthy of all the praise and honor. There is none like You, Lord. You are my strength, Lord. Thank You, Lord. I worship You, Lord, for You are worthy to be praised. My soul loves, Jesus. Saints of God, my soul is ever rejoicing at the love and power of our Father in heaven. The Lord is good. Do you hear me? The Lord is good.

The Bible says, "O taste and see that the Lord is good: blessed is the man that trusteth in him" (Psalm 34:8).

This scripture has come alive in my life since submitting myself to my Lord and Savior Jesus Christ. I had to get out of my own way and stop pointing the finger at others. Yes, I was in my own way. My body, mind, and soul belong to the Lord. I freely give it to Him. It was and still is a choice. The Lord's desire is for His children to prosper even as our soul prospers. Hallelujah!

Father in heaven, help me to express the love, gifts, and talents that You have given me in a way that is pleasing to You and will encourage others to give their lives to You. Lord, it is my prayer that each reader takes away a fresh anointing just as You have given Your daughter. Thank You, Lord, for being on my team. Thank You, Holy Spirit, for comforting me through these hours, days, and years as I patiently wait on the manifestation of Your glory to be revealed in my life. All for Your glory, Lord. Hallelujah!

Saints of God, "O taste and see." Hallelujah! Glory to God. The Lord wants to bless us. He loves us so much. Can you feel Him? He is all around us. He is Omnipresence. Right where you are, you can experience the love of God. Hallelujah! Oh, taste and see! Give our hearts while we still have time. Seek Him while He can be found. Come out, come out, wherever you are. Obedience is better than sacrifice. We most believe the Word of God. Hallelujah!

Just when we think our cup has been filled, then our amazing God shows us that there is more. The Lord's blessing shall overtake us if we would allow Him to come into our lives. You see, I am not limiting God's blessings to just tangible things, but more than what we see, we have His spoken Word that He will never leave nor forsake us. Hallelujah! You see, our feelings come and go depending on what we see, but our Lord wants us to trust Him to keep His Word whether we see it or not. Hallelujah!

The Lord wants us to eat His Word. His Word is the Bread of life. The Bread of life is God's Word. We might not see it, but it is written in our hearts, and the Holy Spirit will bring it back to us to taste and see. Hallelujah! Glory to God. Bless Your name, Lord. It is my prayer that someone is getting this Word right now. I pray that you are being motivated to get up and taste and see that the Lord is good. No, we do not have to stay down—only trust the Word of God. He has given us everything we need in His Word. This is a new day dawning. Will you join me and the many others across this earth in just simply trusting God? Let us keep our belly and eyes full with the Word of God. God is good!

These writings are mere expressions of my gratitude to the Lord for giving me the grace while I experience this journey with you that His glory be revealed through our lives. Remember, His Word will not return back unto Him void. Hallelujah! The Lord watches over His Word. If you have not, by now, accepted Christ Jesus as your Lord and Savior, this is a good time for you repent and give your lives to Christ Jesus. Pause!

Yesterday morning (before leaving for service) upon waking up from sleep, the Lord Almighty placed a scripture on my heart. I didn't know why at the time, nor did I recall the scripture without going to the Word to find it.

The Bible says, "The thief cometh not, but for to steal, and to kill, and to destroy: I am come that they might have like, and that they might have it more abundantly."

I didn't know at the time why, but I knew that it was significant and I needed to meditate on it. No one can teach us like the Holy Spirit, only if we would listen. There I was singing, praying, dancing, worshipping, and communing with the Lord before leaving home and remembering the Lord's sacrifice of His body and blood so that I have life, totally enjoying the presence of God. Hallelujah!

I had anticipated that the day could only get better from that point. It only made sense to produce more good fruit. Right? It really had not dawned on me that I was going to be reminded of that scripture (John 10:10) in just a matter of an hour or so, but God knew what was ahead and had already given me what I needed to know that my Lord would never leave nor forsake me.

Satan gets so disappointed when God's children are expressing their love for the Father, the Son, and the Holy Spirit in any way. The devil will try whoever or whatever he can do to kill, steal, and destroy our joy. Remember, we fight not against flesh and blood. It is spiritual. If we are not careful, we too can be used by the devil to do his dirty work and not even be aware of it. Help us, Lord. Nevertheless, as believers, we must know that our inheritance is in Christ Jesus. That means we are not alone on this journey. We have to remember the Word of God. The Holy Spirit will bring it back to our memory. We have to do our part and meditate on the Word of God both day and night. Let us not give place to the devil because we simply do not understand what God is doing. We have to examine our hearts and do like David and ask our Father in heaven to create in us a clean heart and renew the right spirit for this is the Will of God.

Yes, the devil tried to take my joy by planting negative thoughts in my mind, but it didn't work. No, it didn't work. No, it didn't feel good physically or mentally, but my spirit remained intact. If there is one area that we must stay strong in, it is our prayer life as believers. Help us, Lord.

> And when he was at the place, he said unto them, Pray that ye enter not into temptation. (Luke 22:40)

> And said unto them Why sleep ye? Rise and pray, lest ye enter in temptation. (Luke 22:46)

> And he spake a parable unto them to this end, that men ought always to pray, and not to faint. (Luke 18:1)

Saints of God, it is our responsibility to guard our hearts and ears from our own insecurities or any insecurities of our neighbors. It is one of the most challenging things to do, and that is getting the saints to come together and pray. We are all part of God's body. Let us take heed lest we enter into temptation. Hallelujah!

The last thing that I would like to share with you in regard to this day's experience is that I took my heart before the Lord in prayer and He restored me. I woke up this morning (with my eyes puffy and practically closed) to a text from my husband saying, "Baby, look at your e-mail because we have been given an interview date." Hallelujah! We have won again. God is faithful. I gave it to the Lord, and He restored me and blessed us with our interview date. Glory to God.

This day is so significant. Actually, this is the seventh day that I have been taking communion at home in the presence of God. My husband asked the Lord to allow us to hear from the NVC in regard to our interview date today. Also, the interview date is the Thursday (April 9, 2020) that leads into the Passover weekend. Hallelujah! Also, I have a conference to attend in April 9–10 in Dallas that the Lord placed on my heart to attend. So powerful, this moment is definitely a new day dawning. It is truly happening for the glory of God. I believe God!

March 21, 2020

Good morning, Holy Spirit. I bless Your name, Lord Jehovah. I give You glory. I honor and praise You, Lord. I thank You, Jesus, for all that You have done. There is power in the name of Jesus. I love You, Lord. There is none like You. I take joy in Your name. Hallelujah! Glory to God. Victory belongs to Jesus. Victory belongs to me. I have the victory in Jesus name. Amen.

Saints of God, I totally have to keep it real with you as always. The last few days have been a challenge for me. It has been exactly twelve days since my last writings to you on this journey. Just yesterday, the devil tried me, but the Holy Spirit reminded me who I am in Christ, God's spoken Word over my life, and God's faithfulness toward His spoken words. Hallelujah! These last few days has been like no other. The world seems to be chaotic over this coronavirus pandemic. The body of Christ has been looking more like the world like never before. The media has been feeding this Goliath of a pandemic so much that the whole world's response is in panic mode. Where is the church? Help us, Lord.

Today is a great day to remind myself, "God is still in control and He watches over His Word to perform it." Hallelujah! Saints of God, we are all faced with challenges on this journey to our destiny, but we have to stay focused on the Word of God. Truth be told, yesterday, I almost gave in to temptation of speaking contrary to what the Word of God concerning my desire, but the Holy Spirit stepped right on in and reminded me to just simply remember what the Lord says. As it is written, "when the Lord says yes, no one can say no." Hallelujah! Yes, it is a battle of the mind, but the Word of God reminds us that the Lord did not give us the spirit of fear. The Lord has given us power, love, and a sound mind as it is written. Whose report will we believe? Hallelujah! Church, let us speak over ourselves the Word of God and trust Him. This is our time to rise and shine. Hallelujah! No matter how big the Goliath is in our lives, the Word of God is bigger. Amen. Our Lord Jesus Christ has overcome the world already. Let us also be the example on earth. We are a team. We can do this. Help us, Lord. Saints of God, let us praise our way through it all. The Lord inhabits our praises. Yesterday is only a reminder to stay focused and not to give up on God's promises concerning our lives. It is all for God's glory. Amen.

The world news reported yesterday that the US Embassy in Ghana was suspended from any interviews until further notice, travel restrictions on the airplanes from Ghana to the United States were implemented, and the conference that I signed up in Dallas was also cancelled on April 9, 2020, which was the date of my husband's interview. Yes, the prince of this world is trying it for us all, but I will trust in the Lord with all my heart and lean not my own understanding. It is already done.

HALLELUYAH

I thank You, Lord. Hallelujah! There is none like You, Lord. You are the first and the last in my life. You are the beginning and end of my life. There is none like You, Lord, King of kings, Lord of lords, Lord of hosts, for You alone is worthy of all the praise and honor. I worship You for the rest of my life. I love You so much, Lord. Jehovah is Your name. Glory to God!

Father, at a time when so much is happening in this world, You are still Lord. We have the coronavirus that even Your own children have declared a pandemic in this land. Father, even Your own children are now living lives of fear and have forgotten Your promises. Father, we now see the shape and condition that Your church is in. It can no longer be hidden behind the pulpits or pews. It can no longer be hidden behind smiles or songs. It can no longer be hidden behind prosperity or education. The head is sick. Your people hearts are racing and blood pressure on the rise. The church doors are closed. No hugs. No kisses. No handshakes. Social distancing is the message from the pulpit now. The number of deaths is on the rise. The doctors are baffled and overwhelmed. Everyone is wondering where this massive destructive Goliath called coronavirus came from. Every nation has seemed to come together in search for answers. It is like being in the dark and swinging at a target that You just cannot seem to hit. Where is the church? Where is the power of the church? Lord, have mercy. Help us, Lord!

Saints of God, I have decided to take this time not only to thank God first for what He has already done from the beginning but also to record the condition of the church during the time that the church should be praying and praising God through one of the most trying times of our generation. If you are now reading this, you should be rejoicing and be exceedingly glad for what the Lord has done for bringing you through as well.

What am I saying? I am simply saying what the Lord has already said. We are identified in Christ. Christ is identified in and through us that the world knows our Savior still lives. The Bible tells us to give thanks at all times. It is my prayer that it wasn't you that retreated when the storm came rushing into your city or family. I pray that it wasn't you that heart was starting to fail because of fear. The worst that could have happened through this process is that God's children pass on to glory to inherit eternal life and the unbeliever not get a chance to accept Jesus Christ as Lord. I pray that even today, God's children are spreading the gospel and living a new life in Christ Jesus. Saints of God, help me thank God Almighty for all that He has already done. The Lord is still on the throne. The earth is the Lord's and the fullness thereof as it is written. Hallelujah! This is our opportunity to be the light that shines in darkness. If you are reading this, you have another opportunity to let your light shine and lift up the name of Jesus. Hallelujah! Glory to God. There is none like You, Lord. All for your glory. Thank you, Lord, for another sunny day. Thank you! Thank you! Thank you! Holy Spirit, help us to continue to remember who we are in Christ and give us comfort when we are discourage by cares of life in Jesus name. Amen

April 1, 2020

Praise Yah! Thank You, Lord, for this day. I am blessed because of You, Lord. Your children are blessed. Father in heaven, thank You for reminding me this morning just how blessed we are to have such an awesome loving Father that cares about what we care about. Hallelujah! There is none like You, Lord. Father in heaven, I believe Your word to be true. I trust You with all my heart, mind, and soul. Thank You for being the Lord over my life. Thank You for being the Lord over my family. Thank You, Father, for being Alpha and Omega in our lives. My confidence is in You. Your Word will not return back unto you void, but Your Word will accomplish what it was sent out to accomplish in Jesus name. "Hallelujah!" I praise You for what You have already done. Thank You, Jesus. Amen.

Saints of God, whatever it is that you think you are going through, give it all to the Lord and leave it there. Let us be certain of the Word of God in our lives and focus on what the Lord Almighty has already done for us on the Cross and how our Redeemer lives. Yes, "Our Lord and Savior got up with all power of Heaven and earth in His Hands" as it is written. This is the Word of the Lord. Jesus Christ is our everlasting Father, our Prince of peace, our Counselor, our Redeemer. Hallelujah!

April 23, 2020

Praise Yah! Glory to Your name, Lord. There is none like You, Lord. Wonderful Counselor, Prince of peace, everlasting Father, I love You. There is nobody like You, Lord. Father in heaven, you keep on making a way for me, and for that, I am grateful. I bless Your holy name. Thank You, Lord Jehovah, King of kings, Lord of lords, Alpha and Omega, the beginning and end. Hallelujah! I trust You, Lord. I lean and depend on You, Father. I give my body as a living sacrifice with gladness. I thank You for what You have already done. Holy Spirit, help me. Holy Spirit, continue to comfort and teach me in Jesus name. Glory to Your name, Lord Jehovah. Remember my family, Lord. I plead the blood of Jesus over my husband, our marriage, our children, and family both near and far. By the stripes of Jesus, we are healed. I ask You, heavenly Father, to give Your angels charge over our lives and over the lives of all of Your children. Father, continue to show the world that You have all power in both heaven and earth, Lord. "Hallelujah!" Praise yah. Glory to Your name. Amen.

Saints of God, it is truly a blessing to be living today. Many people are transitioning to their eternal destination daily. It has been a few days since my last writings. Actually, it was my hope, by now, that my husband would have been home. His appointment was set for interview with the US Embassy in Accra, Ghana, on April 9, 2020, at 7:30 a.m. He was scheduled to be the first to be seen, but life happened unexpectantly, and the pandemic has now affected the US immigration all across the land, including Africa. Wow! This was the moment that we had waited so patiently for over a year and a half since we filed our case with USCIS. Lord, no! It was actually happening and then a sudden screeching halt to our plans actually just one day before the interview. We actually received the e-mail that morning, giving notice that the office was closing, lockdown in Accra, and the cancellation of our interview date to later this year. Also, I received a notice from Hilton Hotel where I was planning to attend a prophetic conference held in Dallas the same weekend. All our plans were suddenly halted. What do you do? What can we do?

Well, what we know to do is to continue to trust God. As my husband often reminds me, "God knows best and He has perfect timing." Glory to God. Only God knows how much my husband and I desire to come together. Only God knows. Has it been easy? Well, let's just say I have my days. My husband has truly been awesome and very poise in His stance and faith in God's promise concerning our lives. These situations, or shall I say challenges, have truly been humbling; but once our mind is made up, all we can do is to wait patiently on the Lord to fight our battles and show us the way. "God's timing is the best timing" has been embedded in my heart as a reminder that God is in control. Praise Yah! Today, I have been reading in the book of Joshua, and by the grace of God, I have been encouraged that these battles belong to the Lord and He will fight all of our battles. Obedience is better than sacrifice. Hallelujah!

Saints of God, I would like to encourage you as well to keep pressing, hoping, and trusting in our Lord and Savior for He knows all about our struggles. God is Faithful. Let us continue to walk together with the Lord as He leads us to victory. We have a choice in these matters. Let's continue to make the right choice and stand on the Word of God. God is bigger than the coronavirus. God is bigger than any sickness or disease. We have the Lord God on our side. We will be victorious. We will receive the desires of our hearts. We will have the opportunity to give testimony, so let us continue to wait patiently on the Lord. Let us continue to pray one for another. Let us continue to love and forgive daily. The Lord is the Light of our salvation. Hallelujah!

July 5, 2020

Good morning, Holy Spirit. Hallelujah! Thank You, Father God in heaven. Glory to Your name. My soul rejoices at the sound of Your name, Lord Jehovah. Thank You for Your Son, Jesus Christ, my Lord. Lord, it was You who put the heart for worship, praise, love, and mercy and made a way for me. Hallelujah! Glory! Thank You, Lord, for Your grace. Thank You, Lord, for loving me so. My soul says yes. Hallelujah! Thank You, Lord, for finishing what only You have started. Thank You, Lord, for completing me and sealing me with Your promise. My soul is rejoicing.

Saints of God, I am sitting here on side of my bed just nodding my head from side to side because our God is so good. I am literally at awe this morning, when I think about the goodness of Jesus and the power of the Holy Spirit. Let me tell you how good God is. God is so good that He intentionally, with His whole heart, continues to remind us just how good He is. Hallelujah!

"What do you mean by this, Marcia?"

Okay, I will tell you this morning. Yesterday, both me and my husband were meditating on the Word of God. The Lord has given us Matthew 17: 20–21 to meditate. It blessed me all day long. That some oil is still flowing this morning as I share it with you beautiful people.

> And Jesus said unto them, Because of your unbelief; for verily I say unto you. If ye have faith as a grain of mustard seed, ye shall say unto this mountain, Remove hence to yonder place; and it shall remove; and nothing shall be impossible unto you. Howbeit this kind goeth not out but by prayer and fasting. (Matthew 17:20–21)

Glory to God. Even as I write down the scriptures this morning, I am reminded of God's Word concerning not only my life but also the lives of God's people. Hallelujah! Glory, Lord. I will not fail. We will not fail. This is the word that ignited the fire of God in me years ago. I have been holding on to this word for years. I will not let go of it. I believe it shall surely come to pass. The Lord has reminded me just this morning once again that He has not forgotten us, His children. Hallelujah!

LOOK AT GOD

Good morning, Holy Spirit. Father God in heaven, hallowed be Thy name. There is none like You. Let Your will be done in our lives as it is in heaven as it is written. You are the greatest, Lord. Hallelujah! Glory to Your name. I believe in Your Word Lord. Do it for Your glory. Do it for Your name's sake. It is You, Lord, pulling me through. Thank You, Lord. We believe Your word, Lord. Hallelujah!

Saints of God, I woke up with my mind stayed on the Word of God. It is necessary. It was necessary. It will be necessary. It shall be necessary. One might ask what is "necessary"? Well, it is necessary that we, as believers, exercise our faith at all times. My husband oftentimes says those powerful words to me. They really pierce my soul every time he says those words to me. Now more than ever, I am understanding and consuming those words in my spirit. Let this mind be also in Christ Jesus. Unless I exercise, my health will be stagnant. Unless I exercise, my mood will be shady. Unless I exercise, my future will be limited. So when it comes to our faith in God's Word, why do we struggle so? Are we exercising God's Word in our lives? Am I exercising God's Word in my life? These are necessary questions that we must examine daily in our own lives.

Look at God. When I started writing this morning, I didn't even have a subject. I just merely opened my journal up and started writing. Look at God. He is so perfect, so awesome, and so merciful. Father in heaven, You are so amazing. Hallelujah! Thank You, Lord, for loading Your children with good gifts daily. It is truly a love affair, saints of God. The Lord loves us so much that He reminds us often of His grace and mercy. Grace and mercy are priceless. Wow!

This morning, my husband and I discussed Isaiah 6:8 and the subject was "send me." This is our response to God's question. "Send me, Lord," should be our response daily as we exercise our faith in God's Word daily. "Send me, Lord," is what our Father is looking for from His children. How many times have we experienced the love of God? How many times have we experienced the presence of God? How many times have we experienced breakthroughs and miracles of God? I know, countless times right. Yes, right.

So, after taking an inventory of our lives, what is our response today? I do not know about your response, but my response today and each day thereafter is "send me." Hallelujah! How can we not go out to tell a dying world about Christ Jesus? How can we not tell of His goodness and mercy? How can we not tell the world that our Lord God Almighty, our Father in heaven, loves them so much that He gave us Himself for our ransom that we may believe on the name of Jesus by faith and that He is the only begotten Son of our Father in heaven who died for our sins and resurrected by the Spirit of God with all power in His hands. Yes, the Lord will give us our heart's desire, but we have to continue to honor Him by continuing to delight ourselves in Him. It does not stop when we received our desires. We have to honor the Lord with our desires. Amen.

IT'S NOT OVER UNTIL GOD SAYS IT'S OVER

July 10, 2020

Good morning, Holy Spirit! Thank You, Father in heaven, for waking me up this morning. Hallelujah! Glory to Your name. Thank You, Jesus. It is not over until You say it's over, Lord. Thank You, Lord, for speaking those words to me this morning. I need You, Lord. I need You to move on behalf of my heart's desire, on behalf of my family. Lord, You have the final say in this matter. I won't complain. I trust You, Lord. You have been so good to me. Hallelujah!

Saints of God, the Lord never said it would be easy. I tell you the Bible is right. Faith is choosing to believe God even when it seems as if the odds are against us. I would not be very honest if I tell you that I do not struggle with my thoughts sometimes, but I am learning daily to lean and trust in God. God is Faithful. God is Love. God is a Spirit. Whose report are we going to believe? Jesus Christ, our Savior, was and is the perfect One without sin. Through Christ, we are made whole. Amen. Through Christ, we have a right to salvation. Through Christ, we are victorious. Hallelujah!

July 18, 2020

Glory to God. Holy holy holy. Lord God Almighty, I thank You. I praise Your holy name. Hallelujah! Thank You, Father in heaven. Thank You, Jesus. My soul is happy for Your glory, God. I love You, Lord. Thank You for all that You have already done, Lord. Have Your way, Lord.

Actually saints, I was planning to testify a couple of days ago concerning how good God is and how much He cares for His children. I am sure by now that more than I can testify of His greatness and faithfulness for His children. God is Good. God is Love. God is Faithful. Hallelujah! It was July 15 when I realized that I had just completed a thirty-day challenge of no added sugar to my diet. I had not realized that, on the fourteenth day, I had met my goal. Thank God for the Holy Spirit.

The Holy Spirit will definitely remind us to be kingdom-minded concerning or dealing with trials and tribulations. We are reminded of the importance of exercising our faith. God truly has a plan for us only if we can just slow it down and listen to His direction and exercise our faith in His Word. The Holy Spirit is our Helper. We discussed "perseverance." We talked about staying the course and persevering through trials by faith that work within us. There it goes again, the concept of exercising our faith. Little did I know that I was only moments from being tested in my faith. You see, the previous day, it was the dilemma of what to do about our taxes. No one anticipated COVID will hit the world as it has, putting a halt to everyday normal living. Nothing in this world is going as usual. So here we are trying to filter our way through and through the challenges and decisions that we are now faced with. No one has the answers these days. One day at a time, we are going to make it. It is not over until God says it is over. We will keep fighting, praying, and fasting until victory is won. Hallelujah!

Heavenly Father, thank You for reminding us of Your Word when it seems like all hope is gone. All power and glory belong to You, Lord. You promised us that You will never leave nor forsake us. Father, You have kept Your promise. Father in heaven, continue to renew the right spirit in us and fill us up daily with Your Word. Father, let Your shield of faith protect us from every fiery dart of the wicked in Jesus name. Hallelujah! It shall surely come to pass. I just found out this morning that some embassy offices are starting to open back up. Lord, we believe Your report. Hallelujah!

JUST A REMINDER

Father in heaven, I know that You have not forgotten about us. I wanted to write this entry to You, Lord, as a personal reminder that we haven't forgotten about You either. There is one word that comes to my mind when describing the year 2020, and that word is REVOLUTIONARY. This year is revolutionary. This is what I have been hearing this week, so I have looked this word up on Google. By definition, it means "involving or causing a complete or dramatic change." I know even the recent changes that I have made to my body and hair are only the beginning of what is about to come forth in my life.

I believe that same leap of faith is happening all across this land in one way or another. COVID has made such an impact on change this year as all in all sectors. I believe this is an introduction to the new era that's being ushered into this land, causing change.

I remember a question that the Lord asked me back in April, "What is more important, your desires or my word?"

My answer is, "Your word is more important, Lord." Hallelujah!

FINAL CHAPTER

And the Lord turned the captivity of Job, when he prayed for his friends: also the Lord gave Job twice as much as he had before. So the Lord blessed the latter end of Job more than his beginning: for he had fourteen thousand sheep, and six thousand camels, and a thousand yoke of oxen, and a thousand she asses. He had also seven sons and three daughters. (Job 42:10–12)

Remember ye not the former things, neither consider the things of old. Behold, I will do a new thing; now it shall spring forth; shall ye not know it? I will even make a way in the wilderness, and rivers in the desert. (Isaiah 43:18–19)

We trust You, Lord. Hallelujah! Amen.

TESTIMONIES

February 19, 2021

The Lord said to me, "There is nothing else that need to be said that has not already been said. It's already done!"

February 24, 2021

My husband called me at 3:30 a.m. to report to me about his interview at the embassy. The phone dropped due to network problems, but I knew God had already done it. He called back at exactly 3:33 a.m. His words were, "Babe, they are granting me the visa. The Lord has done it for us."

Hallelujah!

March 19,2021

My husband journeyed home to his wife. We give you all the glory, Lord. Thank You, Father!

ABOUT THE AUTHOR

Marcia Quainoo is an inspiring new author who has worked as a registered nurse for almost two decades. She has worked passionately in the area of psychiatric nursing for over a decade wherein she was given recognition by her local community hospital for her years of service and compassion toward her clients and community.

Wife and mother of two, she is the last of ten children. Although Marcia seems to have excelled in school and work, like most, she struggled in silence in other vital areas of life until she decided enough is enough. She concluded (after years of failures, fallouts, and fears) the only way is God's way.

Every other treatment is supplemental to the Word of God. The Word of God is medication and life to the believer. We must believe. Everyone will not understand this journey, but those that have a listening ear and know the voice of the Lord will hear what the Spirit of God is saying. The Bible says, "But seek ye first the kingdom of God, and his righteousness; and all these things shall be added unto you" (Matthew 6:33). For the glory of God. Hallelujah!